W9-BJN-584

A PILLAR OF CLOUD

A PILLAR OF CLOUD

THE STORY OF HESSTON COLLEGE
1909-1959

MARY MILLER

MENNONITE PRESS
NORTH NEWTON, KANSAS
1959

COPYRIGHT © 1959 BY THE
MENNONITE BOARD OF EDUCATION
FOR HESSTON COLLEGE, HESSTON, KANSAS
Library of Congress Catalogue Card Number: 59-11477
Printed in the United States of America

TO

THE MEMORY OF T. M. ERB

WHOSE DREAMS AND LABORS

GAVE BIRTH AND DIRECTION

TO

HESSTON COLLEGE

PREFACE

The road taken by Hesston College in its first fifty years was no doubt inherent in its conception. For those who have watched with concern its growth and change, for those who have been a part of its life and learning, and for any others interested or curious, the story has been written.

In recording events I have tried to be objective. In interpreting trends, contributions, personalities, I have perhaps not been. Readers may reserve the right to disagree. The first chapter I felt necessary in order to explain why the (Old) Mennonites were not concerned much earlier about educating their young people. The last one is general because statistics and figures seemed meaningless.

I am indebted to my sister, Nora Mae Miller, who during her last illness prepared much of the information for the charts and graphs in the book; to early students of the college—Rosa Landes Hackenberg, Emma King Risser, Mabel Erb Kauffman, S. N. Nunemaker, and the late Anna Baer Nunemaker—whose reminiscences brought into focus beginning figures, activities, concerns, and privations; to Mabel Erb Kauffman for making available the illuminating, oft-quoted diaries of her father, T. M. Erb; to the critic readers of the manuscript — Earl Buckwalter, D. D. Driver, Paul Erb, John A. Hostetler, Nelson E. Kauffman, Esther Weber, and Gideon G. Yoder; to the Administrative Committee, especially to President Roy D. Roth for encouragement and counsel, and to the other members — Daniel E. Kauffman, Paul Bender, Justus G.

vii

Holsinger, and John P. Duerksen; to Katie Ropp, the college accountant, for help in locating facts and figures; to Melva Kauffman for frequent piecemeal reviewing of the manuscript; to the typists—Norma Jean Martin, Mildred Slagell, and Martha Oswald—for their patience and competence; to Ruth Horsch and Joyce Hathaway for their repeated proofreading; to Dorothea M. Eigsti for the enrollment data; and to Paul A. Friesen for the art layout.

Mary Miller

Hesston College
March 31, 1959

INTRODUCTION

Paul Erb

After fifty years, histories have to be written. For the majority of living people cannot remember back fifty years to the beginnings of things, and the number of those who can steadily grows smaller. And memory and oral tradition are so untrustworthy that after fifty years, or even a shorter span, they cannot be trusted without corroboration. The old man who is sure of what he remembers is occasionally surprised at the evidence from primary written sources.

And so it was necessary that Hesston College should have, in her jubilee year, a written account of how she came to be and of how she fared through her first five decades. It is a thrilling story of courageous vision, of sacrificial labors, of the stops and starts ordered by the Lord, of educational accomplishment written into the registrar's records, of trained personality widely used in the work of the church. Because of the influence of Hesston College in the Mennonite Church of the West, and in the whole denomination, this book is an important addition to the shelves of Mennonite history.

The choice of Mary Miller as the historian was a happy one. As student and teacher she has known Hesston College intimately almost from the beginning. She has been a part of the struggling and the achieving of these years, and writes, not with cold detachment, but with the concern of one whose life-work is under survey. Her original style makes this account something more than a recital of facts. She was fortunate in having good source material in the diaries of T. M. Erb and correspondence files for the entire period.

Here is good reading. The oldsters who remember the whole story will read and give their testimony that thus the pillar and the cloud did lead. The younger people will here get the setting of the institution which now is, and will be inspired to carry it on in line with the purposes and dreams of the founders. For the cloud still moves, and the second half-century calls to greater things.

CONTENTS

CONTENTS

xi

I. THE MENNONITE PATH TO
HESSTON COLLEGE

*And the Lord went before them by day in a pillar
of a cloud, to lead them the way; . . .* Exodus 13:21

*But if the cloud were not taken up, then they
journeyed not till the day that it was taken up.*
—Exodus 40:37

To understand why the Mennonites saw the need of educating their young people so late and so reluctantly, one must
follow the general course of their history. Their early leaders
and founders—Felix Manz, Conrad Grebel, Menno Simons—
were scholars of influence, educated in the best universities of
the time—in Basel, Vienna, Paris. They were masters of Greek,
Latin, and Hebrew, and men of convictions so urgent that
they must needs write, project, and preserve them.[1] So late
as 1750 Christopher Dock, a prominent Mennonite school
teacher near Germantown, Pennsylvania, produced upon request "the first elaborate educational treatise in America."[2]
Why then, did they lose this vision—the feeling of need for
higher education? For almost two hundred years they with-
drew. The cloud settled down over them and they shrank in
fear and suspicion from any inroads the tentacles of higher
education occasionally made into their security.

A public debate with Zwingli in 1525 gave birth to the
Anabaptist movement.[3] In 1536 Menno Simons, the recognized
founder of Mennonitism, threw into this movement his force,
his clear convictions, and his unflinching loyalty to the Word of
God.[4] The Anabaptists through their insistence that adult bap-

1

tism is a clear command from God to those born into His Kingdom, brought on themselves the wrath of the state, in its federation with the Roman Church and later with the new Protestants, in persecution surpassing "in severity the persecutions of the early Christians by Pagan Rome."[5] Re-baptism became a crime. "To give food and shelter to the re-baptized became a crime."[6] "The Duke of Bavaria in 1527, gave orders that the imprisoned Anabaptists should be burned at the stake, unless they recanted, in which case they should be beheaded. . . ." "Thousands sealed their fate with their blood." "Armed executioners and mounted soldiers were sent in companies through the land to hunt down the Anabaptists and kill them on the spot without trial or sentence. . . ." In Southern Germany the number of mounted soldiers hunting them down was increased from four hundred, to eight hundred, to a thousand. The count in charge of the persecutions in the Palatinate exclaimed, "What shall I do? The more I kill, the greater become their number." In 1529 the Reichstag, the National Legislative Assembly of the German Empire, passed an edict demanding that "every Anabaptist and re-baptized person of either sex shall be put to death by fire, sword, or in some other way. . . ." Menno Simons said, "The men in authority . . . ask only whether one was baptized. If the answer is in the affirmative, the sentence is already pronounced and he must die."[7] "Berne, Switzerland appointed 'Mennonite-Hunters' or 'Chasers,' promising rewards for every Mennonite captured."[8]

Needless to say, Mennonites became fugitives seeking seclusion, ever in search of places where they would be left alone. Their resolute belief that participation in war is a violation of the teachings of Christ intensified the persecutions and the

2

urge to isolate themselves. In Holland, in Russia, in Alsace, in Germany they lived in quiet for short periods; but ever and anon the question of military exemption arose, and those who stood firm saw the pillar of cloud before, leading on to new spots where they hoped to live unmolested.

As early as 1662, almost with the first settlers, Mennonites came to America. In 1683 more came by special invitation of William Penn to settle near Germantown, Pennsylvania.[9] In America new lands, unsettled territories ever lured them on. In the move westward, Mennonites were in the front rank of pioneers. In Virginia, in Canada, in Ohio they moved in on raw lands and established homes before the Indians had moved on. In Illinois, and on through Kansas, Nebraska, the Dakotas, Washington, Oregon the Mennonites were among the first to stake claims and set up their sod shanties or log cabins.[10]

The cause for this continuous search for isolation is obvious. They had not lost their fugitive complex. They were suspicious, fearful of the state, of other churches. Their convictions, yet different from those of the people about them, might again at any flare-up bring persecution down upon them.

The outcomes, too, are obvious and natural. They became passive and unaggressive, avoiding contacts, seeking only to be left alone, accepting the position of underlings rather than manifesting as did their founders the authority of their convictions and the dignity of their mission.[11]

So, for almost two hundred years in America, they lived in a fog that blocked vision. They plowed lands, they built homes and supported families; they did these tasks well— better than most—and they continued, insofar as possible, avoiding contacts with the state and with the world outside their own circles. Is it any wonder then that when the ques-

3

tion of higher education began edging in, Mennonites shook their heads in fear and suspicion, for education was under state control, and was not the state their old enemy? And other churches, did they not teach compromise? Education, was it not new, and were not all things new beset with danger? As education edged its way into the church, would it not engulf their children and sweep them out into the world? Not until near the end of the nineteenth century did the cloud begin to lift and the pillar clear itself out of the fog "to lead them the way."

Gradually during those last few years of the past century, new life stirred (Old) Mennonite thought. Spirits emerged from their long hibernation and shook themselves. The world was at their door. Did they not owe it something? Did they not have a mission to minister to it; and how could they do it most effectively? Forthwith began a period of new enterprises and organization. Within thirty-five years they had organized an Evangelization Board, a Mission Board, a Foreign Relief Board, a Publication Board, and a Board of Education; they had established mission stations in India, in Argentina, in Chicago; they had started a hospital in La Junta, Colorado; a publishing house in Scottdale, Pennsylvania; a number of children's homes and old people's homes; and three schools —Goshen College, Hesston College and Bible School, and Eastern Mennonite School.[12]

This forward movement, especially in the establishing of schools, was not by unanimous agreement. Suspicion of education was strong and deep. Time and circumstances and a realization of the inevitability of its coming, no doubt proved more convincing than the reasoning of the more progressive. Voices from the period evidence the onward march. The

4

pillar indicating direction of movement began to take shape clearly.

> Much has been lost to the church because well-meaning parents have mistaken their highest duty. They have been taught from little up that the greatest of all duties was to save and provide for their own. . . . All week long they toiled faithfully and steadily, not only to drive the wolf away from the door but to lay up for a rainy day.[13]

> Perhaps the most vital and perplexing question confronting the church is that of education. The problem is causing increasing concern in proportion as we are realizing the significance of education as a factor in determining the moral and religious life of our young people.[14]

> There was a time when parents had the liberty to send their children to school or keep them at home, but that time is past. Compulsory education in most states has been extended to the high school. . . . It is therefore not a question to decide whether they shall send their children to school but as to where they shall send them.[15]

> Our young people will have an education and if we cannot give it to them in well-guarded schools of our own, they will go out into other schools and get it, and according to past experiences we need not expect more than a small percentage of them to return to the church.[16]

> This is an age of education. We may stand aloof, and oppose it, but it will come just the same. If not through our own schools, our young people will go out into other schools, and many of them will be led astray. Many bright young minds have been lost to the church by going out into worldly schools to acquire an education.[17]

> We believe that ample provision should be made for the education of the rising generation. These educational institutions should be controlled by the church.[18]

> Outside of the lessons learned in the classroom, there are advantages to be gained by going to school that cannot be overestimated . . . . It will enlarge chances for happiness, . . . give higher ideals of life and people, . . . give stores of good things to think about, and enable . . . to rise to clearer heights.[19]

5

The schools are the church's most powerful instrument in working out her mission.[20]

On such a wave of thought, the pillar of cloud moved on into the Middle West to the founding of Hesston College.

The entrance arch to the Hesston College campus built by the academy graduating class of 1920 under the supervision of Noah Oyer, sponsor.

II. ESTABLISHING "A SCHOOL IN THE WEST"

. . . thou leddest them . . . by a cloudy pillar; . . . to give them light in the way wherein they should go.

—Nehemiah 9:12

In the *Gospel Witness* of October 23, 1907, appeared this notice: "An entire carload of brethren and sisters from Kansas passed over into Colorado last week to attend the conference at La Junta."[1]

In the November 13 issue of the same paper the pastor of the La Junta congregation had this item: "On the morning of October 16 at the Kansas-Nebraska conference much important business was brought up and acted on, a report of which will appear in the papers."[2]

In the same issue appeared a report of the conference held at East Holbrook Church, October 17-19, 1907.

> Question 6—Would it advance the cause of Christ to establish a school somewhere in the West, in which Bible work is made a specialty?
>
> Resolved, that this conference believes that the cause of Christ would be advanced by establishing such a school with a consecrated faculty strictly in the order of the church, and that we request the Mennonite Board of Education to take steps to establish a school somewhere in the West.[3]

The light was on! The pillar was taking form, moving, indicating direction. Through the vision of Mrs. S. B. King, who had sensed the capabilities of young people and had handed the question to Bishop T. M. Erb even before conference time, the idea of establishing a church college had been

7

planted.[4]   Many early students of Hesston remember Mrs. King's hospitality and her impassioned life and testimony.

Nurturing the idea, cultivating it, seeing that it became firmly rooted and grew on into action in spite of hesitation, objection, conflict, and fear of possible consequences—this task fell to one man alone, one whose energy, whose persistence, whose indomitable faith and labors stood like a rock through all the discouragements, inaction, and conflicting counsel of the next two years. T. M. Erb's duties during those years were multitudinous. He was in those pre-automobile days *the* bishop, the shepherd in charge of the scattered congregations in Kansas, Colorado, Oklahoma, and Texas. Because these congregations were new and untried, differences, problems, disagreements arose; and his services were required often. He was the tie between the east and west sections of the church—between the conferences, activities, institutions on the west side of the Mississippi River and the various boards and organizations on the other side. He headed the committees that launched the La Junta Sanitarium and the Kansas City Mission; and he was held responsible for them. In a General Conference report of August 26, 1909, appeared this statement:

> Bro. T. M. Erb of Newton, Kansas, was appointed to investigate *all* our church institutions and to report to our next meeting, telling what he saw, what he thinks of the institutions, and giving recommendations if he sees proper to do so.[5]

From the time the question of "a school in the West" was proposed, T. M. Erb would not let the idea lie dormant. He kept it astir in the church mind. In November, accompanied by supporting brethren, he carried the conference resolution to a meeting of the Mennonite Board of Education at Kokomo, Indiana. In the same month appeared this note in a report of the Board:

A movement has been started by the Kansas-Nebraska conference looking toward the establishing of a church school somewhere in the West. The Mennonite Board of Education appointed the brethren T. M. Erb, George R. Brunk, and J. E. Hartzler as a committee to inquire into the advisability of the movement.[6]

T. M. Erb, the founder who received the Western School vision and labored to realize it.

The committee was scattered. T. M. Erb lived on a dairy farm near Newton, Kansas; J. E. Hartzler was an active evangelist, at the time attending school in Chicago; George R. Brunk lived at Protection, Kansas, and was averse to spending time in letterwriting. By December 2, T. M. Erb had letters in the mail to his committee:

> . . . I have been thinking of three things to investigate upon: viz., location, money, and prospective students. The latter I found is the easiest. Many are already waiting to enter such a school and would like for us to have it ready to open by next fall. . . . I am not much alarmed about securing a location, but I am a little dubious about the money.[7]

The committee agreed to meet in May. In the intervening months the chairman collected data. In his diary, February 2, 1908, he recorded,

> Went to Peabody this afternoon. Had a meeting in the town hall tonight about the proposed school in the West. Citizens of Peabody want that school and they are going to work to get it!

On May 8, 1908, he noted, "In evening met the commercial club at Newton with reference to our Western school. They are going to take up the matter among themselves."[8] George R. Brunk reported in one of his brief notes, "One Bro. here in Comanche will give 80 acres. Not that I think this is the place. I only report the offer."*

In May the committee met, visited various congregations "to get the sentiment of the brotherhood," received "a number of invitations for locations . . . to the extent that things looked very favorable;"[9] and in June, 1908, at the annual meeting of the Board of Education at Kokomo, Indiana, the committee reported its findings. The resolution passed by the Board practically assured continued action.

> Whereas there is a demand for a school in the West and whereas we believe that such a school would be a benefit, be it resolved, that five brethren be elected as a Western School Committee, the president of the Board of Education being Chairman. Said committee with the faculty committee of the Board shall find a Head and also a Business Manager and location for such a school. The Western School Committee shall elect an Executive Committee, which shall erect buildings suitable for a Bible School and Academy.
>
> Such Executive Committee shall be subject to said Western School Committee till the next meeting of the Board.[10]

On July 11, 1908, T. M. Erb recorded in his diary, "To town again this afternoon, talked with W. J. Trousdale and Dr. Axtell about locating the College at Newton or Trousdale."

*The only note mentioning the offer of my father, Noah E. Miller, Protection, Kansas, to "the school in the West."

On August 11 the committee appointed by the Board came—
John Blosser, president of the Board of Education, chairman;
J. E. Hartzler; T. M. Erb; C. D. Yoder; and S. B. Wenger.
They visited the colleges at McPherson and Lindsborg and
began the study of six location offers:

> Peabody: 160 acres near the town at $75 per acre plus a do-
> nation of $6000.
> Canton: A donation of 80 acres, "a good alfalfa patch."
> Hesston: A donation of 80 acres near the town plus about
> $7000.
> Trousdale: (Now Zimmerdale) A donation of 40 acres plus
> another 40 acres at $50 per acre plus $3300 cash.
> Newton: A few good places at $125 per acre plus $7500
> cash.
> Harper: A donation of 80 acres.

On Friday and Saturday the committee spent the nights in
T. M. Erb's home, "working on the proposition till 1 o'clock
but could not decide."[11] On Monday morning they met again,
eliminated Trousdale and Harper; and of the four remaining
offers each of the five members of the committee listed his
first, second, and third choices. On the first ballot Newton
received two firsts, Hesston two. On the second ballot Hesston was first choice of all the members of the committee but
one, and he exchanged his first and second choices to make the
vote unanimous.[12] The committee passed this resolution:

> Resolved that after prayerful consideration and discussion
> of advantages and disadvantages of the various places of-
> fered and the welfare of the church in general and the success
> of the school at stake, Hesston, Kansas, was chosen by unani-
> mous vote.[13]

The committee had three more duties: electing an executive
committee authorized "to erect buildings suitable for a Bible
School and Academy," and choosing a business manager and a
principal. One of the three problems had but one answer:
T. M. Erb became business manager, a position he held till his

11

death in 1929. The executive committee chosen consisted of men living in the vicinity.

....................................., Principal of the school
T. M. Erb, chairman
A. L. Hess, Hesston, Kansas
J. A. Cooprider, McPherson, Kansas
M. M. Weaver, Newton, Kansas
C. M. Hostetler, Hesston, Kansas
John Grove, Newton, Kansas

The choice of a principal was deferred and became a long process. The committee "concluded" its work and disbanded, leaving the newly-elected business manager to find a principal from a list of three suggested by the committee. From August to December T. M. Erb carried on a stream of correspondence, asking leaders of the church what sort of man the principal of the new school should be and which of the three men on the list should be chosen. Among those consulted were J. S. Shoemaker; J. E. Hartzler; John Blosser, chairman of the Board of Education; J. S. Hartzler, then business manager of Goshen College; Daniel Kauffman, editor of the *Gospel Herald;* Aaron Loucks, general manager of the Mennonite Publishing House; George R. Brunk; and other ministers in and out of the conference district. Counsel dribbled in—varied, indefinite, and conflicting:

> I yet think we should have looked out our faculty before doing anything else. What good will an 80A farm and $30,000 do us with no men to manage it, and I think that before another step is taken that men should first be engaged because in all my investigation men are a greater problem than money.[14]
>
> The principal should be a competent man, thoroughly seasoned in the school of orthodoxy, one ripe in the experience and needs of the church. I consider the principalship of that school the most important position in the church.[15]
>
> The principal should be a strong educator, or you will not get the strongest students even from your own territory.[16]

12

He must be some spiritually broad-shouldered man who can stand a world of unfriendly criticism. No school has ever started upon the opinions of everyone concerned. ....
.... is not steady enough; students will not accept dash, motion, and emotion as teaching.[17]

.... is a good evangelist—would be out of his sphere as a president.[18]

D. H. Bender has the strongest executive power.[19]

All things considered, D. H. Bender would suit the best of the brethren considered, not only the most able, but your people's choice.[20]

By December 17, 1908, the problem of choosing had solved itself. Two prospective choices had withdrawn their names from the list. D. H. Bender had been prevailed on to accept the position; and practically all concerned, including the two other candidates, had concurred in the judgment of one of the committee men, "I know of no other man who would be better. Glad the matter is decided."[21]

During the last months of 1908 while the choice of principal was "of prime importance" among the church leaders, the school idea had been kept alive on the homeground too. In September, T. M. Erb had gone to the Missouri-Iowa conference. In his diary he noted, "Conference adopted the work done for College at Hesston."

In the report of the conference appeared this item:

What is the attitude of this conference toward the proposed school at Hesston, Kansas?
Answer: We feel to encourage the school on condition that its management, faculty, policy, and work are in line with the Gospel and the Church. If the school will be kept free from popular games, instrumental music, worldly-minded teachers, and other influences which stand in the way of spiritual progress, it shall have our sympathy, our support, and our prayers.[22]

13

In a notebook entitled "History of the Hesston Mennonite School" T. M. Erb recorded, "In Oct. the Conference at Peabody ratified our work."

The Kansas-Nebraska Conference report included this detailed comment:

> Question: What expression of sentiment does this conference desire to give in regard to the government of our proposed school and to the business management?
>
> We suggest the following:
>
> That great care be exercised in selection of faculty, laying out of the plan of the work, incurring expenses, deeding property. . . .
>
> That in case obstacles arise that the way does not seem clear to get the kind of an institution meeting the approval of the church, we advise a halt until the obstacles are removed.
>
> If these suggestions are carried out, . . . the institution shall have our support, our sympathy, and our prayers.[23]

The local committee had begun activities. The members met in the Hess home, then the Erb home; they chose A. L. Hess as treasurer and C. M. Hostetler as secretary; they "walked over the grounds" and "staked out a probable site for the building."[24] On September 1, 1908, they chose "The Western Mennonite School" as a temporary name for the institution; on January 19, 1909, they changed the name to "The Hesston Mennonite School;" on April 27 they appointed Erb and Bender as a committee to select a permanent name; and on July 12 they adopted "Hesston Academy and Bible School" as the name of the institution.[25] By January, 1909, they had adopted the following resolution:

> Resolved, that the School shall be opened in September, 1909, a dormitory to be built first and school to be conducted in this building until the main building is completed, which shall also be pushed to completion as rapidly as means and the work will allow.[26]

14

The committee appointed ten solicitors, each for designated congregations and equipped them with a booklet, "setting forth the history and purpose of the school, a copy of which shall be handed to everyone approached and asked for a contribution."[27]

In response to the advice-seeking letters which T. M. Erb again sent to church leaders, a deluge of tangled sentiment poured in upon him: "I will push as long as there's anything to push, but it looks to me that we are about up against it just now. We don't want something to go up that is a discredit to the church and the community."[28] The "president of one of the leading church institutions gave Bender twelve reasons why he should not go out there and fizzle out with the thing."[29]

A letter from the president of the Board of Education contained these statements:

> I just heard this eve that the Western School went to "sticks"—was ruled out by your conference. If such are the facts, it will not be worthwhile looking farther . . . .
> I can hardly think the purpose was so feeble as that.[30]

Other pointed comments continued coming:

> I am sure there will be problems arise in the course of a few months of the existence of that institution that will stagger the biggest heart and brain in the Mennonite Church.[31]

> One of the church leaders pictured the Western people as 'ambitious, obstinate, wanting to do things!' Are you getting scared?[32]

> If God wants this thing and we are faithful, there's not the least doubt it will go and nothing can hinder.[33]

> On the whole I could not give anyone much encourage-ment for getting money to start that kind of school. I do not know of one family in our church aiming to send their children away to school. . . . To ask a person for money to start that for which he has no particular use would be about

fruitless. . . . It is a question with some whether it is a proper thing for an able minister to leave ministerial work and take the school work.[34]

There are some emphatic protests against starting something so expensive in the West, right on the heels of the big donations for the Western Sanitarium, when there are a number of other institutions already in sore need of funds.[35]

I'd a thousand times rather see that enterprise fail before it starts than see an institution of a worldly sort.[36]

Make it self-supporting from the beginning.[37]

I fear that in calling for $30,000 to begin school on, you will give some people lockjaw.[38]

I favor an immediate move forward. The school ought to start by September, 1909. The longer we put it off, the less liable we are to succeed in the effort to make education and orthodoxy support each other. We should move with caution; the work done should not be of such a nature that it could not be abandoned.

I favor plans which will leave $1000 between amount subscribed and amount to be spent. Leave D. H. Bender out of work that calls for most of the unfriendly blows; the Board should be prepared to do that.[39]

I favor the pay as you go plan . . . think favorably of starting with a dormitory.[40]

Your idea of building according to the pile is a good one. With our present experience, I would never consent to go into debt so much again. It is too wearing . . . . Our credit is good at the banks but it will remain the best if used very little . . . . It will be no obstacle in the way of the progress of the school to be crowded. That will give an excuse for more demands on the people.[41]

We ought to be well prepared for making an opening. It will take some time to overcome a crippled start.[42]

While this melee of ideas poured in, the work on the grounds moved steadily forward. On January 20, 1909, T. M. Erb wrote to D. H. Bender, "Many neighbors would like to do hauling before spring work on farms opens up. We staked off the place so we will know where to haul sand and materials."

By February, solicitors were on the field and the principal from his office in Scottdale had actively tuned in on plans and was urged by the committee to move to Kansas as soon as possible. Joseph Byler was chosen head carpenter and on March 24, "We broke the first ground, with several teams on hand to get away the dirt. This . . . was completed about April 8th . . . . Finished walls on May 4th."[43]

The basement walls for Green Gables. Excavation started March 24, 1909, and basement walls finished May 4, 1909.

The details of the building, now Green Gables, were planned also by the advice of church leaders in the East and West. The business manager of Goshen College, Erb's most constant adviser on building plans, suggested, among other improvements, that there be a storeroom three steps up from the kitchen and a basement room seven or eight steps down. The early students who earned board and room in that kitchen well remember the storeroom three steps up and the basement seven or eight steps down.

After D. H. Bender accepted the principalship, he and Erb were in almost daily correspondence about solicitation of funds, building plans, and the choice of a faculty. On all these matters they sought widespread advice. Leaders suggested they start slowly, cautiously—perhaps with "one strong school man," "at the most two and some local help." Leaders' interest in the choice of "the second man" was keen, and their suggestions many. From the first, Bender favored J. D. Charles, superintendent of the Kansas City Mission since November 14, 1906, minister since May 16, 1908, and formerly a resident of Lancaster County, Pennsylvania.

D. H. Bender wrote on February 15, 1909, "I like the tone of his letter: I would favor his appointment. I think it will not hurt to have two preachers on the faculty of a church school." J. S. Hartzler disagreed, "My suggestion would be that with the business manager preacher, and the principal preacher, you have enough. I suggest a good lay brother for the other man for a number of reasons."[44]

D. G. Lapp favored Charles because "of his high standing in the classics," and Daniel Kauffman because of the several offers Charles had received and refused in Kansas City schools and in the Pennsylvania colleges he had attended.

By March 16, 1909, Bender wrote, "I will write to Bro. Charles and arrange with him to get out the course of study on our way to Kansas next month."

In answer to a letter from T. M. Erb, J. D. Charles wrote on February 11, 1909:

> If you should decide . . . I would be willing to consider a position with the school. Having spent six years in preparation for work of the nature you offer, I feel that I could

be of the best service to the Church in that work. Having declined similar offers simply because they were not with the church, now that there is a possible opportunity to be used in the Church in such work under conditions with which I am in full sympathy, I feel inclined to offer my services.

On February 18, 1909, he wrote again in response to a letter from T. M. Erb, "Salary: We should look for nothing more than a living . . . it seems to me we could do with five or six hundred dollars."

In the same letter he concluded:

> I can easily believe you when you say that you have a harder job than you ever had. But take courage, Brother. *This work is of the Lord. He will give abundant grace and strength.* We are constantly mindful of your arduous task and remember you at the throne of grace. Whether I become a member of the faculty of the New School, or retain my present position, or the Church sees fit to have me do anything else, rest assured that this feeling will not change.
>
> Lost in His Love,
J. D. Charles

On April 15 Bender started for Kansas, stopped at Goshen College "to get all the help I can," and at Kansas City "to plan the course" with Charles. The newly appointed instructor wanted, during the month of May, "to visit at Franklin and Marshall and at the Millersville State Normal School. . . . My visiting at the College and Normal School before they are out of session is highly important."[45]

The local executive board was involved in another problem. The March 18, 1909 minutes record a motion, "that we get a charter for the property of the Hesston Mennonite School."

The new principal wrote:

> I would advise going slowly on the matter of chartering the school as a separate institution. You have a regularly organized board. A few trustees can be appointed and the property deeded to them, the same as trustees of a church.

19

After we have fully considered the matter, we may work out something that will be satisfactory to the people in the West and not hurt our friends elsewhere. I think it would be unfortunate to organize a separate corporation . . . . I believe that when the people in the West fully understand that the Mennonite Board of Education . . . is composed of representative men of the church, the majority of whom hold the same views as we do, . . . there should be no trouble in having that all adjusted satisfactorily. It should be so arranged that the local board has full control of the management of the school, but since we have a general board of education and as it is so representative as it is, I would consider it a misfortune not to be connected with it in a general way.

J. S. Hartzler agreed with Bender:

It seems to me that it would be undesirable, if not an unfortunate thing to have that deed made to anything else than to the Mennonite Board of Education. You can have it put into the deed that the land shall not be liable for any debt of said Board aside from Hesston College nor its proceeds, principal, or interest used for the benefit of any institution east of the Mississippi River.

The minutes of the next meeting of the local board on April 27, the first meeting attended by the new principal, state, "It was resolved that the chartering of the institution be deferred until after the annual meeting of the Board of Education in June, 1909."

On July 12, 1909, the local board decided:

Resolved, that we recommend that the property of Hesston Academy and Bible School be deeded to the Mennonite Board of Education with such provisions as shall protect Hesston Academy and Bible School financially and in the control of its policy, such provisions to be approved by the Western Conferences directly concerned in the management of the Hesston School.

The Kansas-Nebraska Conference report included this item:

The management of the Hesston Academy and Bible School asked for a decision regarding the deeding of the school property.

20

Resolved, that the property of Hesston Academy and Bible
School be deeded to three trustees, located near enough to
the school to make it convenient to do business; the same
to hold this property in trust for the Mennonite Board of
Education who shall have the right to appoint a brother with
power of attorney to act conjointly with the said trustees in
doing business.

In accordance with the conference resolution, the local
board appointed T. M. Erb, D. H. Bender, and J. A. Cooprider
as trustees; and the Mennonite Board of Education appointed
A. L. Hess with power of attorney to act conjointly with the
trustees in doing business.

Green Gables—Hesston College fifty years ago.

Through the coordinating labors of T. M. Erb, the stage
was steadily being set for the opening of school in September,
1909. In a Kansas wheat field where "much rain made it un-
pleasant around the building,"[46] stood a three-story dormitory
with third floor arranged for boys' rooms, second floor for
girls, first floor for school administration, and the basement for
boarding purposes. The chapel occupied the north wing of
the first floor, the library a part of the north half of the west

21

wing, the principal's and business manager's offices the south corner rooms, and three classrooms the remaining space. The building had low-pressure steam-heating from an outside furnace room, water by a gasoline engine and compression tank, lighting and cooking-fuel arrangements installed by the "Ideal Lighting System—a practically non-explosive cold-air gasoline gas,"[47] and "good drinking water drawn from a well directly on the grounds."[48] In building they had heeded the counsel of board members, "had kept good level heads, not taking advance steps without feeling sure of their ground."[49]

Between the school and the little town of Hesston were no sidewalks, and the first two houses north were the Methodist parsonage and the cottage now occupied by Blanche Young. The location had been chosen

> because it is rather an out of the way place where there are not so many inducements to lead the young astray.[50]
>
> because it is especially favorable to moral culture, . . . near enough to cities and railroad centers to enjoy their advantages and yet not so near as to expose students to their evil temptations. Hesston is an ideal site in point of healthfulness, being about 1,500 feet above tide level and having pure air and good water.[51]

The principal, faculty, and staff had been selected and were in preparation for their approaching duties. The principal was a recognized executive out of the center of church activities; "The second man" was an educator, serious and earnest in his devotion to Christ and the cause of education, absorbing during the summer months educational ideals and practices to be transfused into the life stream of the new school. The two helpers were J. B. Kanagy and Stella Cooprider.

The course of study—Bible, Normal, and Academic—had been planned into four terms rather than two semesters. Only two years of any course were to be given the first year of school,

The first Hesston College faculty, 1909-1910. Back row, left to right: J. B. Kanagy; J. D. Charles. Front row, left to right: Principal D. H. Bender; Stella Cooprider.

but announcements assured prospective students that "Special arrangements will be made for more advanced students."[52] A Special Bible Term was announced for the winter months.

Terms and salaries had been arranged. Tuition was $40 per year, board and room $95, and dinners for day students, 15 cents per meal. Five days after school started, the local board

23

changed the dinner price from 15 to 12½ cents per meal.[53] D. H. Bender, the principal, was to be paid $720 per year, his previous salary as office editor of the *Gospel Herald* in the Mennonite Publishing House at Scottdale, Pennsylvania; J. D. Charles $60 per month; J. B. Kanagy $50 per month; and Stella Cooprider was to get her board and room and tuition free; the janitor, J. A. Cooprider, received $25 per month.[54] So late as December 20, the board voted that T. M. Erb, the business manager, should get a salary of $25 per month from the time school began on September 22, 1909.[55] How he was paid for the time, postage, and accomplishments of the two preceding years there is no record.

Not the least of the assets of the school were the citizens of the town, who had encouraged "in word and in deed." A. L. Hess, T. M. Erb's brother-in-law, who had moved to Kansas in

A. L. Hess, who donated the eighty acres of land on which to build Hesston College.

1883 and had assisted in fixing the town site, founding the Hesston State Bank and serving as its president for a number of years, and organizing the town creamery and elevator, donated the eighty acres of land to the school and remained one of its chief supporters and friends during the twelve remaining years of his life. The eighty acres of land was only the beginning of his gifts to the school. Students knew him as "Uncle Abe Hess," who equipped the college farm and kept it producing, provided sidewalks from the school to town, gave frequent watermelon parties and home dinners, a fountain, and $500 donations occasionally. His interest in students and causes was good-humored, kindly, and personal. The name given the town in 1884 suggests the breadth of his influence. Two of his eleven children are still living in the Hesston vicinity and one granddaughter was a high school junior in 1958-59.

The lists of the other friends and contributors to the school have been preserved, are unbelievably long, and evidence the generous support and the confidence of practically every parent and grandparent of our present constituency.

The vision of the founders was clear and their purpose fixed and definite. In the "Circular Letter," handed by the first solicitors to all who were asked for contributions, the purposes of the school were outlined in detail:

> The purpose and aim of the school is as follows:
>
> 1. That it be conducted in full harmony with the faith and practices of the Mennonite Churches, *and under the direct control of her conferences.*
>
> 2. That it shall be considered an institution conducted by the Mennonite Board of Education, with a local board for immediate management.
>
> 3. That its work shall at once aim to cover three courses: Bible, Normal, and Academic. The Normal course to cover sufficient scope to include high school and teacher's grades. The Academic course to be sufficiently full to cover the work

of ordinary Academies and prepare for higher institutions of learning.

4. That vocal music be made a special feature of the school.

5. That the Principal be considered the head of the Bible department; that a strong man, well qualified, be placed at the head of the Academic department, and another at the head of the Normal department.

6. That at least four teachers be employed as members of the faculty.

7. That the members of the faculty shall all be members of the Mennonite or Amish-Mennonite churches, of good standing and thoroughly orthodox in the faith.

8. That it shall be the purpose of the school and especially of the faculty and management to conduct the institution for the good of the church and the cause of Christ, rather than for personal gain or self-exaltation.

9. That the institution—character of work done, financial standing, disposition and purpose of both faculty and managers—shall at all times be open to investigation to properly authorized or interested persons.

10. That a complete report of the work and standing of the institution shall be regularly made to the conferences directly interested.

The questionnaire given to prospective teachers was a detailed list of doctrinal questions. Answers were checked and rechecked by the faculty committee of the Board of Education and preserved by school officials.

Correspondence about prospective students was in T. M. Erb's files. There were letters from parents asking, should I send my boys to Goshen until the new school is "on its feet," or can they get the same studies there? Where will they go to church and will a way to go be provided? What size pillow slips should we send and how long are the windows? Could you find us an overnight lodging place and get us back to Newton if we bring James? Could they earn all expenses and what sort of work is available in a town of that size? What is the best train from Idaho to Hesston? To the question, "How many students do you expect?", asked by T. M. Erb of the new principal, came the reply, "I shall be satisfied with fifty."

Before finishing touches were complete, the opening hour had come. The pillar had loomed clear and high and lighted the way to another milepost.

III. THE BENDER ADMINISTRATION, 1909-1930

And so it was, when the cloud abode from even unto the morning, and that the cloud was taken up in the morning, then they journeyed: whether it was by day or by night that the cloud was taken up, they journeyed.

Or whether it were two days, or a month, or a year, that the cloud tarried upon the tabernacle, remaining thereon, (they) abode in their tents, and journeyed not: but when it was taken up, they journeyed.

—Numbers 9:21-22

THE BEGINNING, 1909-1910

In an evening service on Tuesday, September 21, 1909, Hesston Academy and Bible School opened its doors and was solemnly dedicated. George R. Brunk conducted the service, and S. G. Shetler spoke on "What Seest Thou in Thine House?" T. M. Erb reported a "splendid sermon" and a "large crowd."[1]

September 22 dawned "fair and very pleasant."[2] At 9:00 a.m. the bell, a hand grade-school bell, rang for chapel. In the present first-floor hall of Green Gables, clusters of students broke apart and entered the chapel hall, the present health center. Behind an improvised stand on the platform sat the faculty—D. H. Bender, principal and "head of the Bible department;" J. D. Charles, "the second man" and "head of the academic department;" J. B. Kanagy, "head of the music department;" and Stella Cooprider, "assistant in the sub-academic department."[3]

28

The students, twenty-one of them, gathered in and seated themselves in two or three rows of borrowed camp chairs. T. M. Erb recorded in his diary, "The forenoon was spent in making speeches. Bro. Bender gave a good talk to the students and all."[4]

Sometime during that day the students gathered at the end of the west wing before the door of D. H. Bender's office, now the private apartment of the dean of women. As they entered, one by one or in small groups, the faculty counseled with them, fitted them into the prepared schedule, and set up

D. H. Bender, first president of Hesston College, 1909-1930.

a spirit of comradeship by asking about their homes, their families, their plans. T. M. Erb in his office, the south room in the east wing, sold them books, received payments, and listed accounts.

The three classrooms stood ready with borrowed tables for the teachers, and more borrowed camp chairs for the students. One classroom was located where the reception room now is, one opposite it on the north, and one across the hall where the dean of women's office and living room now are. The library and reading room were on the north side opposite this third classroom. T. M. Erb recorded, "The actual class work began in the afternoon. A good start."

At 4:00 p.m. the faculty met in D. H. Bender's office to revise the schedule to fit needs, to adopt a uniform method of keeping class records, and to agree to meet regularly in the principal's office every Monday evening immediately after the close of recitations.[5]

The initial student body, those who registered the first day school began, merit individual attention.

Entered September 22, 1909

Girls

Name	Address
Basinger, Celesta C.	Moundridge, Kansas
Brubaker, Anna L.	Harper, Kansas
Cooprider, Stella	Hesston, Kansas
Grove, Mary A.	Newton, Kansas
Kiser, Fannie	La Junta, Colorado
King, Emma	Hesston, Kansas
Landes, Rosa A.	Hesston, Kansas
Miller, Fannie	Hesston, Kansas
Schertz, Alta	Newton, Kansas
Wenger, Bessie E.	Versailles, Missouri

Boys

Blair, Levi A.	Hesston, Kansas
Brunk, J. M.	La Junta, Colorado
Ebersole, Roy	La Junta, Colorado
Harder, Reuben	Tipton, Missouri
Kauffman, James A.	Versailles, Missouri
Kauffman, John S.	Versailles, Missouri
Landis, Noah	Canton, Kansas
Miller, Charles	Hesston, Kansas
Miller, David	Protection, Kansas
Roupp, John	Hesston, Kansas
Zook, Walter A.	Larned, Kansas[6]

To this day the first-year dormitory girls have kept a group letter circulating. Emma King Risser remembers that she was the first girl to choose and prepare a room in the dormitory, the northeast one in the north wing on second floor.

The pillar had moved painstakingly forward, past the opening day. The road had been rough and conditions were primitive. In June, T. M. Erb had ordered chairs, teachers' desks, blackboards, and a gong. On September 21, the day before the opening of school, the company wrote, "It was

The first office of Business Manager T. M. Erb, in the southeast room on the first floor of Green Gables, from 1909 to 1918.

31

purely an oversight and we hope you will pardon this seeming negligence on our part . . . the chairs will go forward about October."[7] On October 2, T. M. Erb recorded in his diary, "Carpenters put up blackboards today . . . giving the appearance of schoolrooms now."[8] But not until November 30 did he record, "Our chairs and seats came for chapel and class-rooms."[9]

In preparation was a large basement dining room. It was not ready for use, and besides, there was water standing in it. Until Thanksgiving Mrs. J. A. Cooprider and the girls cooked on a three-burner coaloil stove. The staff and student body ate at one table in the same room the cooking was done, a classroom occupying the present office and living room of the dean of women. The water for cooking, drinking, washing, and cleaning was carried from a pump located where the present pavilion now stands. Bathrooms and toilets were installed during construction but there was no water. Early students report that even after the sewer system was installed,

The first dining room, 1909-1945, in the basement of Green Gables.

it was out of order as often as in order. The outdoor toilets were about twenty feet west of Green Gables.

All early students have vivid recollections of the mud about the building and in the paths leading toward town. "When you stepped off the Green Gables steps you were in the mud," they relate. "There was nothing before and around you but a vast expanse of mud." There were few cars then and no highways. On his business trips T. M. Erb drove to Newton in a buggy through the mud. Students waded mud to the pump to fill their water pitchers and uptown to mail letters. Day students sloshed through mud to school. "Finally," Rosa Landes Hackenberg relates, "to keep us from losing our shoes on the way to school, Abe Hess had Abe, Jr. haul a load of straw to build a sidewalk from the campus to town." S. N. Nunemaker remembers there were wooden planks reaching from the dormitory steps to the straw walk. T. M. Erb recorded in his diary:

> Oct. 20—Mud is very unpleasant around the building.
> Nov. 30—Cesspool and ditches are full of water again. Some water in the basement.
> Dec. 2—Still cloudy and some rain. Never saw such weather in Kansas at this time of year.

D. H. Bender wrote in a letter to the *Gospel Herald* on December 9, "The earth thrown up in excavating was left unleveled, and there are no sidewalks. Only those acquainted with the adhesive Kansas mud can appreciate what we experienced during the rainy spell."

On November 13, 1909, T. M. Erb received a letter from the Missouri-Pacific Railway Company:

> This will acknowledge receipt of your letter of November 11, in regard to a car of cinders for sidewalk across our tracks at Hesston.
> We have particularly noticed the progress of the city of

Hesston, some of it brought about by reason of the fine Academy that has been erected just south of town and want to assure you that our people desire to do everything we can in the way of improving the sidewalks across our tracks to accommodate your people. . . . Mr. Walker will unload a car of cinders at the point designated in your letter with instructions to his section foreman to spread it out and make the walk as soon as he ascertains what is needed.

Hesston Academy and Bible School, including Winter Bible Term students, 1909-1910.

On October 11, T. M. Erb wrote in his diary, "No way to heat the school building so hunted up several coaloil stoves to warm up the classrooms. We can get along but it is very uncomfortable. I worked in the office till 10 o'clock." And on October 19 he added, "Started the first fire in the boiler today."

On November 12, D. H. Bender wrote, "To cap the climax, a cyclone came along, demolished two of our buildings, wrecked two windows in our assembly room and compelled us to use one of the classrooms for chapel services."[10] T .M. Erb

34

in his diary identified the two wrecked buildings as "the hen-house and the outhouse."

Although the winds and rains beat upon the new school, it moved forward undaunted. "There were," D. H. Bender wrote, "precedents to be established; regulations to be adopted; courses of study to be tested; confidence between teachers and students to be attained."[11]

Curricular offerings were not many but solid with content, early students recall. In the academic department, English, Latin, ancient history, Bible, and music were required; the normal course was prescribed by the state; and the Bible course was "a study of the Word, both from the theoretical and practical standpoints."[12]

"There was one microscope in the laboratory, set up in the northeast corner of the basement dining room," S. N. Nune-maker recalls, "and we made our own slides. It was painstaking and slow; but we got experience and knowledge that students now perhaps miss." The earnest young science teacher, J. D. Charles, bred in his students a deep respect for knowl-

An early science class under the instruction of J. D. Charles, in the basement of the Administration Building.

edge and stimulated a seriousness and joy in attaining it. A conviction grew in students that the authority of thorough scholarship and a vitalizing faith in a God who lifted men above themselves gave their instructor a master touch. Students recognized him as an educator with his life sunk in the cause, a thinker whose mind reached on and on for root causes and purposes—for particles of truth to fit together into lifting life patterns.

Two months after the school was started, D. H. Bender had applied for accreditment. The "class C" rating then given by the state was raised to a "B" by the end of the year. At the close of the second year the school was listed "class A."[13]

Two weeks after school began, the faculty met to formulate dormitory regulations. Through almost a half-century the original list has been only slightly altered but parts of it have been through the years executed with gradually diminishing stringency. The list below is copied from the notes of the fourth faculty meeting on October 4, 1909.

REGULATIONS

Students are required:

1. To attend Chapel service daily.
2. To attend Sunday School and church service each Sunday.
3. To refrain from the use of tobacco, profane and vulgar language.
4. To pass to and from recitations in a quiet and orderly manner.
5. To avoid heavy walking, loud talking, laughter, and all unnecessary noise in all parts of the building during recitation periods.
6. To be in their rooms at 8 o'clock each evening except:
   (a) On Saturday, when the time is extended to 10:00.
   (b) When attending religious services.
   (c) When attending meetings at the academy. At the close of such meetings they shall go immediately to their rooms.

36

Study Hours:
    Study hours are from 8:00 to 10:00 p.m.
    Quietness at 7:30 p.m.
    Lights out at 10:00 p.m.

General Rules:
    No visiting is allowed between the sexes in their rooms.
    The reception room is open to students and visitors on all
    permissible occasions.
    Boisterous and disorderly conduct in the building is not
    allowed at any time.
    Students are held responsible for the order and conduct in
    their rooms. Avoidable marring and breaking of furniture
    will be held at students' expense.
    Absolute quietness is insisted upon in the Reading Room
    at all times.

A week later they adopted a system of grades that is very
similar to the one in use a half-century later:

    A—indicates excellent work.
    B—indicates good work.
    C—indicates fair work, of approximately passing grade.
    D—indicates conditional failure, which may be made up by
        special examination or otherwise.
    F—indicates total failure, work to be done again.

    A statement of the grades is sent to the parents or guard-
    ians at the close of each quarter of the school year.

The next year at a faculty meeting on October 4, 1910, a nu-
merical grading system was adopted.

A library was being collected by donations, fees, and offerings. In December, 1910, D. H. Bender sent an article to the
Gospel Herald listing gift volumes and their donors. He concluded, "We further solicit helpful books of any kind our
friends feel disposed to send us. Very gratefully yours."[14] The
Excelsior Literary Society started the first year by the students
charged members fees and gave the money to the library. Until sixteen years later, the library was collected and maintained
by donations and by funds provided by student organizations.

Library and study hall, on the first floor of Green Gables, north of the present office of the dean of women.

On December 15, 1925, the local board first voted, "that we appropriate a budget of $50 (fifty dollars) for library purposes."

On October 3, less than two weeks after school opened, T. M. Erb had recorded in his diary, "Organized a church at Hesston today with 22 members."

A letter in the *Gospel Herald* added:

> At present there are about 22 members who were received by letter and still others who have not received their letters from the home congregations. Bro. T. M. Erb officiated in the services. . . . Sunday School was organized. Superintendent, J. M. Brunk; assistant superintendent, J. D. Charles; choristers, Bro. Kanagy and Roy Ebersole; secretary, Sister Stella Cooprider. Services will be held each Sunday afternoon.[15]

Early students report that on Sunday mornings they attended the town churches, or by riding in rackwagon or walking down the railroad track they went out to "P-A," a rural church originally composed largely of families from Pennsylvania.

38

From the beginning of the institution, religious services have held a prominent place, as the following listing suggests:

> Each Lord's Day a Sunday School and Young People's Meeting, followed by a short sermon ... in the Chapel Hall, on Tuesday evening a public prayer and praise service, a student-organized Christian Workers' Band, a four-week Special Bible Term, during which there will be special gospel meetings to help the lost into the Kingdom and build up the saints.[16]

The first Special Bible Term and evangelistic meetings were under the direction of George R. Brunk and J. B. Smith.

Students as well as faculty had accepted the pioneering challenge and adjusted themselves to existing conditions. There was no gymnasium, no recreation equipment. On December 20, 1909, the local board passed a motion that "We will not have a gymnasium now." S. N. Nunemaker recalls that on Saturday at the beginning of the second nine-week term, he got off "Jerky," the only train going through the town, at the Hesston railroad station and stepped into the mud. Because he was going to boarding school, he had left his farm clothes at home. When he arrived, the boys were in overalls carpentering in the dining room, arranging the newly-arrived desks and chairs, and helping with the farm chores. The students were largely from the farm, accustomed to physical activity. A few were content not to leave the building for months at a time. One first-year student when asked to come out and play replied, "Oh no! my father paid good money to send me; I can't take time to play; I must study." The boys played football, basketball, baseball out in the mud until they were literally covered with mud from top to toe. Inside on third floor of Green Gables they fastened a ball on the pulley that lifted trunks to their floor and practiced athletic skills on it. T. M. Erb noted in his first business manager's report, "Some students worked very cheap about the building. Outside the teachers, the work of janitor, etc., the labor has all been done by the students."

Five days after school began, students organized the Excelsior Literary Society with James Kauffman as president; they listened during the year to far-reaching lectures—"How We Got Our Bible" by J. B. Smith, "The Schools of India" by Lydia Schertz. They enjoyed watermelon parties given by A. L. Hess, Halstead picnics, and hayrack rides in wagons owned by Hess. On November 25, T. M. Erb wrote, "The students nearly all came down to our place for dinner."

On Arbor Day they bought and planted trees or shrubs on the campus and through the year carried water in buckets to keep them alive. Rosa Landes Hackenberg remembers that as she and S. N. Nunemaker each planted a rambler east of the Green Gables steps, he made this dedicatory pronouncement, "May the future students of Hesston Academy be as multitudinous as the rosebuds that shall blossom on these vines!"

Trees and shrubs for Arbor Day planting.

Before the end of that first school year, sixty-seven students had enrolled. The secretary of the faculty recorded, "J. A. Hilty has been appointed to assist J. B. Kanagy in the work of hall manager."[17] In the new catalog issued during the year the administration announced:

> Hesston Academy and Bible School is not a school for boys and girls needing special restraint, but rather for men and women who have enough maturity to appreciate the advantages offered to them and to make the best of their opportunities .... It is not considered wise to restrict the liberties of the trustworthy for the sake of those who are less reliable. Students whose example or influence is injurious or who will not improve their time, are not solicited.

There were, of course, no graduates that first year. The closing exercises of the school were by faculty decision "to be an educational-musical program."[18]

Because the management erected a furnace building "at a cost of $1,000" and equipped a laundry for "a little less than $1,000" and by order of the state, installed a better sewage system and a fire escape, and because the crops on the college farm and among the constituency were an almost complete failure and consequently pledges could not be paid, and because beginning an institution usually requires unforeseen expenses, the year ended with a $10,000 debt on the new school.[19] In his 1913 report to the constituency T. M. Erb stated, "Before June, 1913, the Board of Education assumed $5,150 of our indebtedness on condition we'd pay the rest. This practically puts us out of debt." Concerning the first year of the school, the principal wrote:

> Faculty and students manifested a loyalty and such a degree of interest in the success of the institution that the burden was much lightened . . . this coupled with a deep conviction that God was with the work . . . that His Spirit was directing.[20]

41

The Missouri-Iowa Conference "reaffirmed their former resolution to support the school on condition of its continuing harmony with the church."[21]

The Board of Education at its annual meeting on May 31, 1910, expressed both warning and confidence:

> We are aware that these schools are in the world, and with the winds of popularity beating upon them, that there are disease germs found in the atmosphere; hence great care must be taken not to give any favorable condition for these to grow and increase. We feel it absolutely necessary that these fountain heads of influence be firmly based upon true Gospel principle in all the work and exercises of the schools and in view of these facts we give the following suggestions:
> That in selecting faculty great care be exercised.
> We realize that physical exercise is necessary for the students; but since there are some games and exercises which encourage a mania for sporting which surely saps the spirituality out of those who would follow them, hence we advise that all games and contests which have any other object than needed recreation should be dispensed with.

An added item near the end of the Board's report stated, "The request to put in a four-year Academy was granted."[22]

On the last day of the year 1909, T. M. Erb had written in his diary:

> This closes another year with its joys and difficulties. It has marked quite an epoch in history for me since we got the new school at Hesston built and started.
> May God ever bless it to the furtherance of His Kingdom on earth and the preparation of many for His Glorious Kingdom!

The school had begun its long, long task, had moved forward day by day planning, testing its plans, establishing precedents, building confidence. Above the rough, hard places loomed the pillar of cloud beckoning on; with broadened vision and renewed effort the ready spirits of the early leaders responded to the call.

THE SECOND YEAR, 1910-1911

The second year was not so trackless and rugged as the first; yet progress was not spectacular. Bases had been established; the new school was settling into its home, habituating itself to its functions, its possibilities. The first faculty stayed and new ones were added—J. B. Smith, W. W. Oesch, and Esther Lehman on the regular faculty and Noah L. Good and Martha Shenk as assistants. Organization drew clearer divisions of labor: J. D. Charles became registrar and secretary of the faculty; W. W. Oesch librarian with Roy Ebersole as assistant; Stella Cooprider preceptress; J. A. Hilty assistant in the business office; and T. M. Erb and A. L. Hess were "appointed a committee to look after the working of the school farm."[23]

In its second year the school had become a regular four-year academy. Excerpts from the principal's annual report show curricular development.

> The Academic department has been strengthened by adding one more unit of work to meet the requirements of the Kansas State University for accreditment.
>
> Several school boards made applications for teachers; in fact we had more applications than we were able to meet. Kansas has just passed a law that after 1915 no new teachers will be eligible to teach in the state who have not completed a four-year high school course or its equivalent. Because of this law the prospect for increased attendance in the normal department is promising.
>
> A four-year Bible Course has been added.
>
> A majority of students in all departments took music.
>
> There is an urgent demand for the teaching of agriculture. We are looking for a man with . . . adaptability and . . . technical preparation . . . to begin the work.
>
> The number of volumes in the library has been doubled. Among the free contributions . . . is a set of historical works . . . of more than sixty volumes "by two sisters from Oronogo, Missouri," a good *Encyclopedia Britannica* "by a brother from Roseland, Nebraska," a series of works on the Reformation "by a brother from Versailles, Missouri."[24]

43

The enrollment in September was thirty-eight and by the end of the year had grown to seventy-six. Notes from Erb's diary indicate that student activities during the year included a number of community work gatherings.

> March 24, 1911
> Bro. Bender, A. L. Hess, and myself to Moundridge to look after trees for the Academy.
> April 6
> Fetched two loads of trees to be planted on Academy campus, 733 trees.
> April 7
> This is Arbor Day at the Academy. It was a big day. All the students helped to plant trees and many planted a tree or more for themselves, paying for it. A good many neighbors came in and helped to plant. Afternoon we had a literary program on Arbor subjects and some good music. It was fine.
> April 17
> I was up at the school, planted some trees and worked in the office.
> April 18
> In the office and planted some trees.
> April 19
> Abe Hess and I finished planting the trees this afternoon.
> September 17, 1910
> The students gathered some apples here today for apple butter. They got a wagon load.
> September 18
> Were at Jonas Zook's to help get apples ready for apple butter for school.

There was still no gymnasium. On October 11, 1910, the faculty passed a motion, "That we permit three games: croquet—with a choice of two from lawn tennis, basketball, and baseball."

Religious activities increased during the second year. The Y. P. C. A. was organized with Paul Erb as president, a position he held for the next four years. The association organized evening devotional classes and mission study classes in small groups directed by student leaders. Throughout the Bender administration these groups met regularly once a week and were a live, prominent feature of Y. P. C. A. activity. The

Hesston Academy and Bible School, 1910-1911.

organization also started a Thursday devotional meeting from 7:00 - 8:00, during which all other campus activities were suspended, a meeting which also continued throughout the administration and was alive with spontaneous student expression. There was "practical Gospel work in and about the town as opportunity afforded."[25] A letter to the *Gospel Herald* added, "Our difficulty is not in finding places for the cottage meetings but in visiting all the places that are open to us."[26]

Expansion in accommodations and equipment was almost entirely postponed. Sidewalks were built and $100 worth of laboratory supplies was purchased. The business manager's report for the year stated, "As far as running expenses of the school are concerned, we have come out a little better than even."[27] But the report was not all good.

> Subscribed donations . . . not nearly all paid in. . . .
> Crops not . . . very good. We have not been able to lower
> the indebtedness; what money was collected was needed to
> make up last year's deficiency, to purchase needed improve-
> ments, and pay interest.[28]

To erase the standing debt, solicitors were on the field. The
local board decided "that D. H. Bender make a western trip in
the interests of the church and school."[29]

At home, A. L. Hess and T. M. Erb, who were in charge of
the academy farm, were evidently interested in gathering a
dairy herd. Local board notes contain these items: "M. M.
Weaver gave a cow to Hesston Academy and Bible School;"
"R. C. Yoder of McPherson donated a cow to Hesston Academy and Bible School;" "Hesston Academy and Bible School
received a donation of $55 from A. D. Driver of Versailles,
Mo. for the purpose of buying a cow."[30]

On May 31, 1911, the first graduation exercises were held.
Five students were in the class—Stella Cooprider, Emma Byler,
Allen Erb, Melvin Landis, and John Hilty. Within that group
began a number of tendencies that have persisted through the
history of the institution. Two of the boys in the class married
the two girls; all five of the group grew on into responsible
positions. A copy of their program remains.

Invocation	
Music	Chorus
Oration—Poetic Portraits	Melvin Landis
Essay—Woman's True Sphere	Emma E. Byler
Music	Male Quartette
Address—Man, His Being and Purpose	John A. Hilty
Reading—Cassandra Southwick	E. Estella Cooprider
Music	Class of 1911
Address—Life's Perspective	Allen H. Erb
Presentation of Diplomas	D. H. Bender
Music	Male Quartette
Benediction	

Of the program T. M. Erb wrote in his diary, "Our first

commencement tonight to an overflowing audience. Many could not get in. The program was fine. All good sensible speaking."

The year had given confidence. Students were forming friendships and loyalties that drew them back and others along with them. Those responsible knew their ground and kept their eyes on the pillar of cloud before.

MORE PIONEERING YEARS, 1911-1915

During the next four years, 1911-1915, Hesston Academy and Bible School moved steadily forward in a natural, unspectacular growth. The faculty gained strength in experience, training, scholarship. By 1913, J. D. Charles had received a master's degree from Columbia University after a one-year leave of absence; J. B. Kanagy and Alta Mae Eby were work-

Hesston College faculty, 1911-1912. Back row, left to right: M. D. Landis '11, '19; J. B. Smith; T. M. Erb; W. W. Oesch; Harry A. Diener '13. Front row, left to right: Principal D. H. Bender; Esther Lehman; Stella Cooprider '11; J. D. Charles.

47

ing toward degrees, and J. B. Smith had an M.A., a B.D., and a S.T.D.[31] In 1915, four of the six faculty members— D. H. Bender, J. D. Charles, J. B. Smith, Alta Mae Eby, J. B. Kanagy, and M. D. Landis—were "taking advanced work in higher schools during the summer vacation."[32]

Enrollment fluctuation during the four years was due to two opposing factors, growing confidence in the school and crop failures in the Middle West. Consecutive enrollments were 99, 122, 106, and 107. Numbers in graduation classes grew from eight to twenty-six.

Curriculum adjustments during these years were continuous and scholarship standards rigorous, as faculty meeting notes attest.

> Dec. 13, 1911—Reconstructed Normal Course to meet state requirements.
> Sept. 10, 1912—A motion was passed that all students be required to take a spelling test. Those falling below 75% and not below 60% may have a second opportunity. Those falling below 60 shall be required to take it at least one term.
> Sept. 8, 1913—A penmanship class was decided upon.
> Sept. 14, 1914—A motion was passed that Academy students be required to have three years of Latin or four years of foreign language if the course was missed, one of which must be Latin.
> A motion was passed that—students be required to take one and one-half years of algebra.
> Jan. 14, 1914—Resolved that we require a grade of 85% for graduation:
> 1. For the general average of the student's grade.
> 2. As the average for the last year's work.

In 1912-1913 the institution was fully accredited by the State Department of Education, and the University had since the end of the second year given it a "Grade A" rating. Normal training graduates received state certificates renewable for life. In the fourth year another dream of A. L. Hess was realized. After several visits by a representative from the state department, an agricultural course was begun, "following the order prescribed by the state for textbook, laboratory, and practical observation work."[33]

Library and study hall.

New equipment was being added to the laboratory—"three microscopes donated by friends in Pennsylvania and Illinois"[34] and "apparatus recommended in the Chute's Physics and Wentworth and Hill's Manual."[35] On March 25 Erb wrote, "Helped test samples of milk from my cows in the laboratory by the agriculture class."[36]

The Bible curriculum had grown. There were two-year and four-year course arrangements. Students were encouraged to choose Bible electives, "thus making the Bible prominent in every department."[37]

On March 15, 1915, the faculty made a decided move forward. "A motion was carried unanimously that we offer a year of college work, subject to the approval of the local board."

While the school was growing out of its infancy, student

49

energies blossomed into natural and more varied activities. In 1912-1913 a ladies' chorus was organized and directed by George Hostetler. In the same year the school chorus "rendered a cantata, 'David the Shepherd Boy,' to about 700 people. Well rendered. Much appreciated."[38] On June 6 "The chorus class went to McPherson in six automobiles to render the cantata, by request of the brethren there."[39]

An early class social.

By faculty consent class organizations were effected and each class was allowed a social and an outing annually. On January 15, 1914, the faculty decided "to launch a school paper, *The Hesston Academy Journal*; that M. D. Landis be the editor, and that he be supported by three contributing editors." To get class themes accepted and published in the new school paper became a competitive student activity.

The Excelsior Literary Society was divided into two new ones, the Advance and the Angelethian. In the spring of 1915 the Webster Debating Society was organized "to offer more advanced work and special training in debate and argumenta-

tion."[40]   For almost half a year only men were eligible for
membership in the new debating society.   At least four times
a year these societies staged public programs that drew community crowds.   In 1911-12, at least three of the programs
were debates—"Resolved that the U.S. is advancing in civilization."[41]   "Resolved that the farmer is a greater benefactor to
society than the manufacturer;"[42]   "Resolved that coeducation
is an improvement over systems in which the sexes are separated."[43]

In athletics there were cautious moves forward.   At the beginning of the third year "Students presented a petition for a
place to exercise in inclement weather.   It was decided to provide them a place."[44]   At the next faculty meeting "Plans for
a gymnasium were considered."[45]   The local board on November 21, 1911, "decided that we build a gymnasium 28 by 40
by 12 feet and that the business manager (T. M. Erb) and
the treasurer (A. L. Hess) look after the building of the
gymnasium." On December 1, 1911, T. M. Erb wrote, "Had
no school today so the boys built the Shed to exercise in.
Frank Roupp was overseer carpenter. They did not get through
with it."

The Y.P.C.A. saw new possibilities.   Group prayer meetings
were held each day on both floors of the dormitory.   These
daily prayer meetings continued through the Bender administration and by many students were given credit for vital character changes.   A Volunteer Band was organized and held meetings each Sunday morning at 5:30.   In 1913-14, evening mission and Bible study classes were conducted by eight student
and faculty leaders—Ida Kreider, Siddie King, Howard Stevanus, Grace Cooprider, Noah Oyer, Mary Ramer, Paul Erb, and
Alta Eby.

Green Gables and the half-moon drive lined with cedars
purchased and planted by individual students.

While student activities expanded, officials were vigilant and
alert. Repeatedly they had been warned by conferences, by
bishop advisers, and by the Board that education led into dan-
gers. By keeping a steady hand on controls, they planned to
avoid complications. Faculty meeting notes show the tighten-
ing tendency in blanket faculty supervision.

Oct. 11, 1910
Motion: That the athletic association be subject to the
faculty. Carried.

Nov. 19, 1911
Motion: That the executive committee of the Y.P.C.A.
appoint a social committee on approval of the president of
the . . . school.

Jan. 11, 1912
Literary society constitutions considered and approved.

Oct. 2, 1912
Alta Eby appointed as chairman of public literary committee.

Nov. 5, 1912
Motion: That each class be granted the privilege of having a social.
Sept. 7, 1914
J. D. Charles was appointed faculty member of the Athletic Association.

Concerning the new school *Journal* the local board "moved and carried that we elect T. M. Erb business manager and M. D. Landis editor of the proposed school journal and . . . appoint the business manager, the editor, and the principal a committee to make all appointments necessary and to have charge of the publication."

At the annual meeting of the Board of Education on October 13-14 a committee was appointed "to examine all textbooks and to submit a list of approved books from which texts may be chosen—and to examine libraries."

A new setting, new habits, and new people had set up restraints that for a time curbed natural tendencies and impulses in students. Gradually these wore away and the faculty saw new needs for precautionary measures.

Jan. 21, 1912
Discussed advisability of locking doors at 10:00.
Sept. 10, 1912
Decided to put up a doorbell and take off the door to the reception room.
Oct. 29, 1912
Reports from a number of other institutions were read with a view to making a demerit system.
Nov. 20, 1912
That three unexcused absences or three occasions for official discipline during a term (9 weeks) places a student on the demerit list.
That upon evidence of diligent application and good deportment a student's demerits may be removed by vote of the faculty at the end of a term.
Nov. 2, 1914
Moved that a Sunday afternoon quiet hour be observed between 2:30 and 5:00.

Regarding discipline the principal stated in his annual report for 1913, "... the growth of the school has added new and grave problems in ... keeping all in line with the Word and the Church." And in his report for 1915 he said, "The discipline of the school during the past year was rather a pleasure than a burden. No serious difficulty arose and no student was officially reprimanded or disciplined."

Laundry, heating plant, and smoke stack west of Green Gables.

The growth of the school plant was not marked during these early years. The $10,000 debt incurred the first year was paid by 1913. Only small utility constructions were added—a cistern near the dormitory, the "exercise shed," concrete walks to the pump and the laundry, a "new barn" to replace the shed which had stood just west of the dormitory furnace room,[46] two more wells, a septic tank, and each year more trees. By 1913 there were 1,000 trees growing on the campus, and "a pavilion was constructed to shade the pump at the approach to the building."[47] When that pump was removed in 1916, Howard

Stevanus covered the well with a concrete slab and inscribed on it, "God is our Rock. Christ is our Life." The inscribed slab was removed and replaced with a new sidewalk in 1955.

Sidewalk inscription, under the pavilion.

After paying its initial debt, "the institution met its running expenses from its direct income until 1921-22."[48] The first commencement program had made evident the need of a new building. Of the May 13, 1911 program T. M. Erb had written, "Our first commencement tonight to an overflowing audience. Many could not get in."[49] The next year he wrote, "I

Class of 1915, M. D. Landis, sponsor.

55

was to Hesston getting seats ready in the park for our graduating exercises."[50]   And before the end of the 1912 commencement he added, "Evening a shower at Hesston—We could not have services in park so had them in Assembly Hall."[51]

For four years, unless spring rains prevented, all commencement programs were held in the Hesston Park, which at that time had a grandstand, green grass, and a number of trees.   By January, 1913, the local board began plans for a new building by appointing A. L. Hess, T. M. Erb, and J. A. Cooprider as an investigation committee.   Voluntarily a subscription was started in the community, and by June, 1913, almost $6,000 had been pledged.   In the *Gospel Herald* appeared a commendatory letter with the names of six influential bishops attached.

4/16, 1912

To Whom this may Concern, Greeting:

We desire to call your attention to a question in which we feel sure you are already interested. The question that comes closest home to us is the well-being of our children. It is our prayer that they may not only be able to win their way in this world, but that they may be won for the Kingdom and spend their lives in the service of Him who gave His all for them. We are exceedingly anxious that those of them who desire an education be permitted to get it under the most favorable circumstances possible, and with as little danger to their spiritual safety and well-being as possible.

The question as to whether a church school among us is a help or a hindrance to the cause of Christ and the Church is still an experiment. We are hoping and praying that it may be a help. At any rate, we want to give our schools a fair trial and vigorous support for the time being, so that they may have every opportunity for proving themselves worthy of our support. Without our support they are sure to fail; with our support they may mean much for the future Church.

The immediate object of this letter is to speak a word in behalf of supplying the present needs of Hesston Academy and Bible School. That school has had a steady growth from the start, and not counting the cost of building, has been a little more than self-sustaining. But they have outgrown their

present room and another building is necessary. We have all
confidence in the spiritual soundness and professional ability
of the faculty, and appreciate the hard struggle they are making to keep the school where it ought to be spiritually and
in loyalty to the Church. We therefore declare ourselves in
hearty favor with the idea that they should be heartily supported in their undertaking and given every opportunity to
prove that a school rightly managed is a real blessing to the
Church. To this end we favor giving them a liberal support
in erecting another building.

Wishing you the choicest of God's blessings, we remain,

Your brethren in faith,
S. G. Lapp.
Daniel Kauffman
J. M. Kreider
A. I. Yoder
Joe C. Driver
S. E. Allgyer

Jottings from the diary of T. M. Erb, who spent a great part
of the year, 1912-13, at home recovering from the results of an
accident, indicate the progress in building plans.

Dec. 30, 1912
    Abe Hess was here this afternoon to talk over plans for
school building.
Jan. 26, 1914
    Abe Hess and the architect here to submit plans for the
school building.
April 10, 1914
    The Local Board moved to begin work on new building
as soon as possible, and progress as fast as finances warrant.
April 17, 1914
    Drove stakes for new building.
April 29, 1914
    Breaking ground for the new building. Abe Hess and a
few men are at it.
June 15, 1914
    Frank Roupp started to put in forms for foundation on
college building ... but the men were driven in by the rain.

By August 6, 1914, when the principal and business manager
made their annual report, the foundation was in, $8,000 had

57

been subscribed, and the school was ready to send out solicitors. Clear and high rose the pillar of cloud before, and the
air was alive with the imminence of expansion.

During these years a calamity had struck a chief supporting
pillar of the school. When T. M. Erb installed the new "Ideal
Lighting System" in the first school building, he also put one
into his own home. When he came home on the evening of
September 6, 1912, during the first week of school, he discovered the light plant was giving trouble. While he, with his
seven-year-old daughter Elva, was in the basement investigat-
ing, an explosion occurred. He tried to put out the flames en-
veloping the child and was burned critically about the face,
hands, and legs. Later he wrote in his diary, "Daughter Elva
died—burned to death because of my carelessness. May God
forgive me."

After three months in the hospital he returned home and
because "all the grafted skin had come off and his legs were
a mass of sores," he called for an anointing service.

> On January 10, 1913, the ministers met with other brethren
> and sisters in his home, after agreeing that God would and
> could heal according to His promise. Bro. Erb was anointed
> with oil, and the prayer of faith for his healing was offered
> by a number of brethren. Bro. Erb was perfectly submissive
> and contented, willing to wait God's time for healing or de-
> parting . . . but ready to receive a miracle if God wills.[52]

In May, 1913, T. M. Erb wrote to the *Gospel Herald,* "It is
now nearly eight months since the accident and I am not able
to walk yet." During the next two years he walked on crutches
and did much of his office work, but his legs never healed. On
June 17, 1915, his right leg was amputated.

In these six years, especially during T. M. Erb's illness, a
close brotherhood had developed among the early leaders of
the institution. A. L. Hess did Erb's office work for him and

often drove to his home to consult him. D. H. Bender and J. D. Charles came "to talk textbooks," "to talk over school matters," "to talk class and teacher arrangements."[53] They came to take him to the doctor, they met one another at trains after a journey, they wrote almost daily letters to one another during absences. When J. B. Smith was ill, J. A. Coopriders took the six Smith children into their home for a week.[54]

A. L. Hess had stood ever ready at the call of need. He supervised the school farm and helped with all campus constructions. The first issue of the *Journal* reported, "Teachers and students are always glad to see the smiling face of 'Uncle Abe' about the buildings and campus." And the October, 1914 *Journal* added, "Uncle Abe Hess never disappoints the Academy people. He entertained us at his home with a load of watermelons." In 1914-15 he "purchased two little yellow mules, Jenny and Molly."[55] Jenny lived long and became a tradition; she pulled the college milk cart for years and was photographed and eulogized in the 1939 *Lark*.

The college barn and dairy about 1920 and Molly and Jenny, the team of mules given the institution by A. L. Hess.

Another adopted uncle and staunch friend of the institution was R. J. Heatwole, a singing evangelist, with a long beard, who appeared now and then, gave students samples of his homely philosophies in chapel, sang solos for them or duets with M. D. Landis.[56]

Two lesser happenings of these years seemed important at the time. In February, 1914, during an icy blizzard with a temperature of 5 degrees above zero, the heating plant burst. For one afternoon the students lived in the kitchen and dining room to keep warm and were then apportioned out into faculty and community homes until repairs came three days later. In the spring of 1913 three students and a teacher became ill with typhoid. T. M. Erb wrote in his diary, "Must make arrangements to boil drinking water."[57]

These six academy years instituted many of the spiritual bases that still stand—cooperation with the church and conference, a cautious scrutiny of innovations, a recognition of the Bible as the measuring standard for truth and manner of life, a strong devotional life, and a stern individual sense of duty and industry and discipline. Evident in these early years was a vision that stirred men to vigilance for opportunities that led on to wider usefulness—that made them eager to follow the pillar of cloud on to college stature and the construction of the Administration Building.

YEARS OF FINDING ITSELF, 1915-1930

Curriculum expansion was rapid after the first six years. In 1915-16 one year of college work was given; the next year two. The principal wrote in the September, 1916 *Journal*:

> It is claimed that it requires about seven years for an institution to establish itself and its principles and get into a position to run smoothly and attain real proficiency. What our work has been in the seven years the school has been in

existence, we will allow those who have been in touch with it to say, but we are now in position to do even better work in the future.

By 1918-19 the school became a four-year college and was named "Hesston College and Bible School," its principal, D. H. Bender, became the president, J. D. Charles the dean, and its courses were organized into wider departments—col-

J. D. Charles, instructor, 1909-1923; first dean, 1918-1923.

lege, Bible, and academy. The same year the college conferred its first degrees on M. D. Landis, Chester K. Lehman, and Noah Oyer. Of the college work of these early years the president wrote:

> The work of the first two years of this course is standard and that of the last two years, while it does not meet all the requirements of standardization, is nevertheless of a commendable quality and our graduates have experienced little difficulty in entering graduate schools and universities.[58]

61

During the years, 1918-1927, when Hesston College was giving four years of college work the institution played a crucial part in training the leadership of the church at large. At this same time the only other college under the Mennonite Board of Education was undergoing a period of readjustment. The fact that the Hesston College graduates of these years hold so many prominent leadership positions in the church today is no doubt a result of this set of circumstances.

In 1924-25 the academy was reorganized "to conform to a junior-senior high school whereas we find it difficult to meet all the requirements in the certification of our teachers under the four-year plan."[59] In the same year the junior college was for the first time given temporary accreditment by the state university. "The one consideration making the accreditment temporary was an unsatisfactory financial situation."[60]

By the next year, 1925-26, because of a $10,000 drive then in progress, the junior college was re-accredited for two years. In 1927-28 the first junior college class was graduated. The same year and for the first time academy subjects were grouped in departments and graduation requirements expressed in terms of majors and minors.

The same year the college asked the Mennonite Board of Education for permission to give a four-year Bible course. In answer to the request from the school the Board replied, "Hesston College may give a four-year theological course provided it does not imperil its junior college standing with the state."[61] The Board at the same meeting deferred a decision on granting degrees for the course, requested that in instituting the course financial obligations be not increased; at the same time it appointed an educational policy committee to "cooperate with the schools in the study of educational standards and policies, to study demands for educational programs in the light of the needs of the constituency and of the standards of accrediting agencies, and to study educational policies of other churches and schools."

In 1928-29 the new four-year Bible course was given.

> Fifty per cent of it regular liberal arts work and fifty per cent study in the Bible and Christian Work. . . . The entire course will be equivalent to a four-year college-course; but, because of its specialized nature, will not merit the regular B.A. degree. The liberal arts portion of the course will merit graduation from the junior college department.[62]

The same year the first a cappella chorus consisting of "faculty, friends, and community alumni" was organized; and the first extended chorus tour was taken to churches in Colorado, with Paul Erb as director.

In 1929-30 the junior college was again accredited for one year by the State University and the Kansas Board of Education, and again the institution requested authorization to grant degrees for the four-year Bible Course. The Board moved

> that Hesston College be granted permission to give a certificate for the four-year Bible Course with the understanding that if degrees are later offered, the same may retroactively be conferred upon those who in the meantime conclude the course.[63]

While the pillar of cloud tarried upon the institution during these years of groping and experimentation, the junior college emerged, was repeatedly accredited, and remained. The fuller dreams of the founders were not realized in their time. Three of the early leaders—A. L. Hess, J. D. Charles, and T. M. Erb—were during these years taken from the institution by death; and two of the evolving leaders, Noah Oyer and Edward Yoder, who had been nurtured to constant vigilance for the pillar of cloud before, were called away by other church institutions. Then in 1930, when the college was already beginning

63

to feel the depression, came the end of the Bender administration.

Changes accessory to the development of the curriculum—heritages now taken for granted—were at the time tasks of great moment. When college work was instituted the search for a fitting name for the school began. The local board wanted "an appropriate name suggesting that the Bible and Christianity have a prominent place; a name convenient to use; if it were not for the length, "Hesston College and Bible School" would have pre-eminence, but for the sake of brevity a shorter name is favored."[64]

Other suggestions were "Shiloh College," "Carmel College," "Berea College," "Hesston College." Finally the local board sent two choices—"Berea College" and "Hesston Bible School" —to the Mennonite Board of Education for approval. The local board was asked to make the final decision.

> After considerable discussion it was decided to use the name, "Hesston College and Bible School," as the full legal name of the school; but with the understanding that in the general business of the institution, the shorter name of "Hesston College" be used.[65]

The Mennonite Board of Education approved the choice, and a *Journal* writer concluded:

> We have reason to believe that the name now adopted will meet with general satisfaction. There is little change from the original, it expresses fully the scope and purpose of the school, it retains the part that suggests the location, and since the people of Hesston and vicinity have done a great deal toward establishing and supporting the institution, it is but right that the name "Hesston" should be retained.[66]

In 1915-16 for the first time one unit of Bible was required,[67] and the next year an advanced six-year Bible course was given to match the development in the college curriculum. In a written report to the constituency the dean, J. D. Charles, formulated the objectives of the college:

> The purpose of the college is . . . to provide the instruction, activities, and atmosphere that will develop all the powers of the individual; to introduce him to the great fields of knowledge; to cultivate true Christian character; and to prepare him to take his place in life as a useful member of society.[68]

On May 11, 1920, T. M. Erb wrote in his diary, "In office. Worked on seal and motto for school." On June 1, he added, "The motto—'The Truth Shall Make You Free'—was accepted." Because the phrase was the 1916 graduating class motto, Noah Oyer, who was the class president, used it as the title of his graduation speech and later suggested it for the school motto. T. M. Erb had devised the seal; and on January 6, 1921, both the motto and the seal were adopted.

Hesston College motto.

In 1919-20 the school paper was named the *Hesston College Journal*. In 1918 the commencement *Hesston Academy Journal* was for the first time edited by members of the senior class; in 1922 it was given a different format from the regular issues, and in 1925 it was named the *Lark*.

In 1922 the State Superintendent of Public Instruction in

Kansas issued a notification that no school would be accredited whose faculty or students used tobacco, nor any certificate granted to individuals who used it. The faculty took grateful note. "Edward Yoder was appointed to write an expression of appreciation to Elizabeth Wooster, state superintendent, for her faithful execution of the law prohibiting the use of tobacco in schools."[69]

In the 1923 *Lark* the president wrote, "Nine (students) entered Near East Relief, where one gave his life, this being perhaps as large a number as went from any other Kansas College. Another served with the Friends Reconstruction Unit in France." In recognition of the sacrifice of Menno Shellenberger, who contracted a fever in the Near East and died there, alumni and friends started a Menno Shellenberger Memorial Fund.

In 1923 the Mennonite Board of Education formulated more definite policies. Its schools should prepare students for work in the church rather than for secular positions; their curricula should be standardized; there should be, unless local conditions demanded a four-year college, only one four-year church college with other schools supporting it; curricula of schools should be arranged to correlate; there should be "standard courses in uniform sequence."[70]

A dramatic event of the year, 1923-24, was the planting of the Boston ivy on the north side of the Administration Building in a ceremony immediately preceding the college senior class program. Chancy King, the class president, gave "The Spade Address" admonishing his classmates and the audience gathered north of the building, "that we pattern our lives after the ivy in its outstanding characteristics—by first planting our feet firmly on a safe foundation and then climbing to get the light necessary for growth."[71]   A part of the class sang "The Ivy Green" as they planted the ivy that until the recent dry summers had covered two sides of the Administration Building.

"The Ivy Green" planted originally on the north side of the Administration Building by the college class of 1924.

In 1924-25 occurred the first "Preachers' Week," the first commencement rendition of the "Holy City" in which alumni and ex-students participated, the introduction of a system of scholarship points devised "to insure standards of scholarship" —an ulterior motivation made more necessary perhaps because the fervent, commanding spirit of J. D. Charles had disappeared from the scene.

In 1925-26 I.Q. tests were first introduced, the school year plan was changed from four terms to two semesters, and the original building was named "Green Gables"—a name suggested by Anna Loucks of Scottdale, Pennsylvania, because the gables were green and because the book, *Anne of Green Gables,* was then popular. A 1925 *Journal* note states that in the

67

state normal training examinations Hesston College had never had a failure; while in that year alone of the 3,000 who took the examinations only 2,000 passed.[72]

In 1926-27 students and faculty families competed in the composition of a college song. Various efforts were given trial and the present college song written by Ursula Miller was adopted. The same year a teacher placement committee was appointed, normal training students began observation and practice teaching in outlying schools, and the college sponsored a series of University of Kansas lectures on "Dr. Johnson and His Circle," "The Joy of Writing," "Our English Bible," "The New Poetry," "The Times of Queen Elizabeth."[73]

In 1927-28 the Y.P.C.A. started the first scholarship fund with the condition that those who were later able should repay, but the money given those who afterwards went into mission work should be a donation. By 1928-29 the faculty began to curtail extracurricular activities.

The regular student enrollment during the twenty-one years of the Bender administration rose from 67 to 248; the total enrollment including Special Bible Term students climbed to a peak of 278 in 1927-28; and the Special Bible Term enrollment itself rose from 14 to 60 by 1919-20 and then receded to its original number by 1930. College enrollment by 1930 had increased from 8 to 66. The number of academy graduates varied from 5 in 1910-11 to 52 in 1921-22; college sophomores from 10 in 1925 to 28 in 1928; and four-year college graduates from 2 to 7. For eight years, 1919-1927, the school gave B.A. degrees each year except one, 1924-25, the year the junior college was first accredited.

During the twenty-one years, a number of faculty members came and went, but a few were absorbed into the life of the institution and gave it its tone and character. The original leaders with one exception remained with the institution until death took them away—A. L. Hess on December 30, 1920; J. D. Charles August 30, 1923; and T. M. Erb January 25, 1929. D. H. Bender, the president of the school during its first twenty-one years, resigned during the summer of 1930.

Among other faculty and staff members who during the Bender administration gave a substantial number of years of service to the institution were J. B. Kanagy and J. B. Smith 7 years each; Alta Mae Erb 18 years; Paul Erb 13; M. D. Landis 17; Noah Oyer 10; S. E. Miller 12; Siddie King Oyer 6; Margaret Horst, Paul Bender, Edward Yoder, and D. D. Driver 8 each; Esther Good 11; J. L. Shellenberger 13; M. E. Hostetler 10; Gustav Enss 7; S. M. King 6; Mary Miller, Ruth Bender, I. E. Burkhart, and Andrew Glick 5 each. A long-term dean of Eastern Mennonite School, Chester K. Lehman, and the dean of Goshen College Biblical Seminary, H. S. Bender, acquired their first teaching experience at Hesston College. Among those who stayed by the institution far on into the next administration were Alta Mae Erb, who taught 31 years; Paul Erb 30, J. N. Byler 16, D. D. Driver 34, Mary Miller 23, Milo Kauffman 26, and Maurice A. Yoder 29. The four teachers named last are still with the college.

In the continuous collaboration and interaction of minds required to promote the progress of an institution, a number of discerning personalities gradually towered above the surface. The president, D. H. Bender, was the ready mediator who understood conflicting views, accepted them, and molded them deftly into one general view. His resourceful, conciliatory powers were widely used—between church and school, at conferences, in family and church difficulties, in sponsoring the institution, and in solicitation and discipline. In 1912 he was ordained a bishop, and for a number of years he wrote the adult Sunday school quarterlies. In 1917 he was sent into the northwestern United States to explore the territory for prospective settlers, he investigated the Southwest with a view of opening a mission among the Mexicans, he was on the Hospital Board then concerned with establishing the first Mennonite hospital, and as president of the Joint Committee on Emigration of the Mennonites of South Russia he traveled widely on land inspection tours with railroad immigration agents. In problem-solving he was the accepted counselor. He kept the new school before the church eye in apt word pictures and convincing summaries. He was until his resignation in 1930 a capable executive who with the confidence and support of his staff and constituency established Hesston College and guided it on its first twenty-one uphill years.

During the lifetime of J. D. Charles, his spirit perhaps more than any other dominated the growing institution. To him Christian education became a passion, a drive that swept before it human inertia and incidental obstacles. To each task he gave the whole of himself and students found his passion for impersonal, objective knowledge contagious. He taught Latin, philosophy, Bible, science, education; he was for years pastor of the college congregation; he gave scholarly, informative lectures on "Fallacies of the Theory of Evolution," "Archeology and the Pentateuch," "Agriculture of the Bible," "History and Cultivation of the Apple," "Values of Higher Education," "Religions of the World," "The Educational and Cultural Value of Discipline and Government," "Mohammedanism in North Africa," "College Athletics." Many of these lectures were by demand printed in pamphlet form for distribution. His " 'Fallacies of the Theory of Evolution' was reprinted by a number of colleges from Pennsylvania to Oregon;"[74] and his "College Athletics" was acclaimed "by numerous letters from other colleges as a comprehensive study of athletic principles."[75] In 1919 he addressed the Council of Church Colleges of Kansas on "The Importance of a Vital Christian Faith for Teachers in a Denominational School," and again in 1922 on "Ideals and Objectives in Christian Education." He gave the commencement address for the first class graduating from the La Junta School of Nursing and lectured in the Hesston Town Hall series. He was sponsor of all college graduating classes during his lifetime, teacher in the college for fourteen years, and dean for four years.

The summer of 1922, one year before his death, J. D. Charles spent " . . . completing an entirely new registration system—the result of a thorough investigation of systems used by other schools and colleges."[76] In June, 1923, he went as a delegate to a conference in North Dakota; on July 4 he returned home ill, and in August was taken to the hospital and his condition reported critical. D. H. Bender and Noah Oyer were at the time participating in a conference in Canada but returned home on receiving a telegram of J. D. Charles' illness. They arrived before his death, which occurred on August 30, when he was only forty-five years old. His funeral at Hesston was held September 2, 1923, and his body was then sent to Pennsylvania. Noah Oyer accompanied the family to Chicago, and J. B. Kanagy from Chicago to their destination.

The J. D. Charles Memorial Program held in the college chapel October 1, 1923, consisted of

Devotional—T. M. Erb
Life and Work of J. D. Charles—D. H. Bender
How the Life of Bro. Charles Has Helped Me—Open Response
Hymn—"Arise, My Soul, Arise"—Led by Paul Erb

The hymn chosen was direct and telling—one J. D. Charles had made a theme song in a series of meetings he had conducted the previous year. The sentiment of the hymn was typical of his manner of living. In open response, students spoke of his austere patrician qualities, which upon acquaintance unfolded into warm, lifting friendliness; his devotional life, rich in intimacy with Christ and closeness to God. Noah Oyer, who had charge of the open response period, closed it with a question—"driving the lesson of J. D. Charles' life directly home" —"Is *my* life an invitation to others to follow Jesus?"[77]

A part of D. H. Bender's speech on "The Life and Work of Bro. Charles" follows:

> When a mere boy, he had a peculiar bent for books. It was something new in the Mennonite Church at that time to go to college, but after completing the course in the local high school and later being graduated from the State Normal School at Millersville, Pa., he took his A. B. degree at Franklin and Marshall College and several years later his A.M. degree at Columbia University.
>
> In our work here at Hesston he was what I called the heart of the school. . . . He had for the last number of years held both positions of registrar and dean. Bro. Charles was methodic, systematic, exact almost to being critical. He was a prompt man. He would not undertake anything he had not carefully studied through. This characteristic was always evident on the occasions that he conducted services in chapel. When he got up to speak, he was exact, practical. To him life was a tremendous proposition to be taken seriously, not lightly. He expected students to come to recitation with work well prepared. If any student had a good reason for not being prepared, he was always considerate, almost lenient, if the student came to his desk before class to explain. But he had no mercy for the "bluffer," and no student ever "bluffed" his way through any of Bro. Charles' classes.[78]

J. D. Charles' private library was sold under the direction of Noah Oyer to students who had taken work under him and used many of his books. D. H. Bender in a letter to the *Gospel*

Herald on "The Death of J. D. Charles and Its Effects on Hesston College and Bible School" had to assure students and the constituency that Hesston College would go on even though J. D. Charles was not here.[79]

The two men who did perhaps more than any others to bring Hesston College into existence and to build, maintain, and support it during the first two decades were T. M. Erb and A. L. Hess. Their plans and labors have been much referred to in these pages. Because they believed that a well-equipped, attractive physical plant generated a higher grade of life and work, they gave their time and effort to provide such a plant. For thirteen years A. L. Hess was at the beck and call of the institution with counsel, time, hospitality, and funds. The

The A. L. Hess family. The youngest daughter, Helen '28, '30 (Mrs. Herbert Kaufman), is in 1959 the fifth grade teacher in the Hesston Grade School.

president called him "undoubtedly the warmest friend of the institution during the first thirteen years of its existence."[80] Two years before his death he developed heart trouble and gradually grew weaker until his death on December 30, 1920. His funeral was held in the college chapel with D. H. Bender and J. D. Charles in charge. A third building, a girls' dormitory, planned and begun the year after his death, was to be dedicated to him. Because of the financial depression that followed, the building was never completed. Not until 1947 was Hess Memorial Hall finished and dedicated.

T. M. Erb's multitudinous responsibilities followed him through the years. For twenty years he was president of the local board, for a number of years president of the town council. He was chairman of the board of trustees, of the building committee, and custodian of finances, records and legal documents. To him we owe the preservation of the materials pertaining to the early history of the institution.

After his accident in 1912, although rheumatic pains were

A girls' physical education demonstration.

frequent and severe, he continued his services to the institution until the year before his death. During his last years a cancerous infection developed in his remaining leg and after a year of absence in 1928-29 he returned home to have the leg amputated. He did not survive the operation. On January 24, the day before his death, he recorded in his diary, "It looks pretty much like I may not get well. For the sake of the family I'd like to get well, but if God wills I'm ready to go any time." His memorial service in the college chapel on February 5, 1929, consisted of

Devotional—J. B. Smith
His Home Life—Emma Risser
As a Man of the Community—S. N. Nunemaker
As a Member of the Local Board—Earl Buckwalter
The Relation of the Business Man to the College—Edward Yoder
Student Appreciation—J. N. Weaver
Twenty Years as a Co-Laborer—D. H. Bender

The president of the college spoke of him as "the leading factor in making the school possible. He first got the vision and suggested the need."[81]

An apt tribute to him is a poem entitled "Blessed" by a student.

God saw him climb the steps of life
    With brave, aspiring tread;
His valiant shoulders strong through strife
    Calm sunshine on his head.
God heard his earnest, leaning prayers,
    And knew the souls he led.

God loved his steady, upward look,
    His ready hand and strong.
A faithful son! God closed the book
    And looking on him long,
He lifted him above life's cares
    To join the heavenly song.

Alice Kauffman, 1929

75

S. E. Miller, instructor in biological science, 1920-1932; assistant business manager, 1928-1929; second business manager, 1929-1930.

S. E. Miller, who was an instructor in biological science and agriculture from 1920 to 1932 and served as registrar from 1924 to 1929, was assistant business manager during T. M. Erb's year of absence in 1928-29. He succeeded T. M. Erb as business manager and served in that office until the end of the Bender administration.

A number of early teachers and officials were much beloved and are unforgettable: J. B. Smith for his exquisite humor and his encyclopedic fund of information; M. D. Landis for his natural teaching abilities, his aesthetic appreciations, and his dramatic readings of the "Book of Job;" Siddie King Oyer for her warm, impartial friendliness during her years as matron; and Paul and Alta Mae Erb whose long strenuous years of service will later be treated in detail. The J. A. Cooprider family had moved from their farm in McPherson County, Kansas, to help the school in varied capacities—Mrs. Cooprider as matron and cook; and Mr. Cooprider as superintendent of buildings and grounds, business counselor, and member of the local board.

Two men, Noah Oyer and Edward Yoder, early shouldered official responsibilities and grew into stature during the administration. Noah Oyer entered the academy in 1912, became hall manager and superintendent of buildings and grounds in 1914, was graduated in 1916 as president of his class, and in 1918 became a member of the faculty. When he was called to Camp Funston in October, 1917, during World War I, D. H. Bender and J. D. Charles made several trips to the camp in an effort to get him discharged. As an academy student he had organized a

M. D. Landis, English and history instructor, 1911-1928.

77

primary Sunday school in the Hesston Congregation and had started some years later the first summer Bible school in the Mennonite Church. Besides initiating Christian education organizations now taken for granted, he installed and constructed on the campus various accessories essential to a school plant. "He solicited the funds for the Master Program Clock, purchased from the Seth Thomas Company and designed especially to announce by bells the classes and other programs of the institutions." He installed the clock, and a year later "assisted by Paul Bender and Joseph Graber" he put into the dormitory a "secondary clock connected with the large master clock." In 1920 as sponsor of the graduating class he inspired the first class gift—the entrance arch with the sign "Hesston College" above it. The semicircular walls flanking it and the retaining walls with the iron railing, running to meet the half moon entrances, were a part of his original design, and were built by the next two graduating classes. "Brother Oyer and the class did most of the work of construction. They even made the cement blocks that were needed to be a peculiar shape to fit the semicircular design of the walls."[82] The walls have since been removed, but the arch remains.

In the summer of 1920 Noah Oyer was planning to go to Princeton Theological Seminary the following winter. Because he knew that the health of A. L. Hess was failing and that from "the founding date" "Uncle Abe" had often spoken of adding a fountain or aquarium to the college campus midway between the two buildings, Noah Oyer decided it should be built while "the benefactor of the school could enjoy it." "'Uncle Abe' offered to pay for all the needed material; students and others donated labor."[83] Noah Oyer and Paul Bender measured painstakingly to discover the shortest line from Green Gables to the Administration Building. On the spot

The aquarium.

midway between the two, students under the direction of Noah
Oyer began work on the aquarium. On June 29, 1920, T. M.
Erb wrote in his diary, "Turned water for the first time into
the aquarium. Fetched Abe Hess over this afternoon to see it."

From Princeton, Noah Oyer wrote to the president:

> It seems to me we ought to be adding more scholarship
> to our faculty. Of course, if nothing above an A. B. can be
> found in sympathy with the church, the A.B. is the one to
> use; but if an A.M. is at all available, I hope you will be
> able to find him . . . .
>
> We ought to build up our standard of scholarship on the
> part of the faculty as quickly as is consistent with all issues
> involved.

After the death of J. D. Charles, Noah Oyer became registrar
and head of the Bible Department, and the same year was
ordained as a minister. In February of that year he organized
a Mennonite Historical Society, served as its president, and
formulated its objectives: to encourage study and research in
Mennonite History; to disseminate facts concerning the history

79

of Mennonites; to establish and increase a Mennonite Historical Library at Hesston College.[84]

Noah Oyer, second dean, 1923-1924.

In the summer of 1924, one year after he had become dean, the local board faced a new problem. "After a lengthy and serious discussion" the board passed this resolution:

> Inasmuch as the church through her General Educational Board is urgently calling for Brother Noah Oyer to serve as Dean of Goshen College, we, the Local Board of Hesston College and Bible School, hereby declare our reluctance in giving up a faithful servant and efficient worker; if, however, the church so calls and he has the conviction that he can be of larger service to the cause of education in the church by accepting this call, we freely and fully release him, and pray God's blessing upon him in his new position.[85]

In 1924 Edward Yoder was elected dean. During his four-year leave of absence, 1924-28, Paul Erb served as acting dean. In 1928 Edward Yoder received a Ph.D. degree from the University of Pennsylvania, returned to Hesston College, and for five more years served the institution in official capacity.

The scholarship bred in these pioneer years had in it a stoic quality belonging peculiarly to a bygone day. Perhaps such stamina had developed because the spending of hard-earned money for such a will-o-the-wisp as education was in Mennonite circles yet new and very serious; perhaps because education above the elementary grades was not then a general practice, the school consisted chiefly of older students and those who had strong intellectual drives. The difference in the curricular emphases no doubt played its part—the strenuous, objective, cultural nature of the course offerings of that day in contrast with the practical, introspective, psychological slant of the education of our day that concerns itself primarily with the self and its advancement and with doing rather than being. Or perhaps persistent effort was more common then because children in the homes of that day were taught to accept long, disagreeable, and difficult tasks as a part of principled living.

An index to the standard of scholarship maintained in an institution is the nature of its extracurricular activities. The motto of the Webster Debating Society was "There is no excellence without great labor." They met each week to debate questions like "Resolved that the U.S. Government should recognize the Russian Soviet Government;" "Resolved that Asiatic immigration should be permitted on the same terms as European;" "Resolved that Ireland should be granted independence;" "Resolved that the Battle of Marathon had a greater significance to future civilization than the Battle of Arbela." Once a month they met in live sessions to study and practice parliamentary law. Both college and academy societies staged a series of intersociety debates and oratorical

Faculty and students, 1922-1923. College and academy seniors in the rows behind faculty.

and reading contests. One intersociety program in the days before students from other countries came to Hesston College, consisted of readings of the twenty-third Psalm in thirteen different languages. In the *Journal,* class papers were published on "The Development of the Papacy," "The Influence of Geography on History," "The Sponge Industry," "Menno Simons —The Life With a Challenge," "The Decline of the English Drama." Students listened to public faculty lectures on "How We Got Our Numerals," "How We Got Our English Bible," "The Wonders of Electricity," "Farm Tenantry," "Rome," "Economy in the Learning Process."

Whether so disciplined a scholarship was a natural product of the more austere philosophy of the times or whether it was nurtured by the persistent impassioned teachings of the faculty is difficult to say. However that may be, a strenuous campaign for vigorous application permeated the institution. Excerpts from J. D. Charles' lectures and echoes of ideas like his indicate strength and persistence in bearing aloft high standards.

> Anyone attending school merely as a place to acquire athletic fame or in which to have a good time should promptly be driven out, even though he is making passing "grades." He is injuring himself. He is injuring his fellow students. Hundreds of young men and women are ruined by being allowed to "dally" four years in school. They read an hour or two a day and persuade themselves they are working when in fact they are only acquiring habits of laziness and self-indulgence and a small surfeit of knowledge which is often worse than ignorance. When they get out of school, many continue to dally and indulge themselves .... The student who has not learned to work ... who has never sweat intellectual blood ... has wasted his time.[86]
>
> * * *
>
> It becomes the duty of such a Christian school to look after the character of its students. The few words I have to say are based on profound conviction. Such a school is not a reform school, nor a hospital for rakes, nor a luxurious lounging place for idlers. It is a place consecrated to truth

83

and virtue. It is therefore an unpardonable sin for the atmosphere of the school to be long polluted by the foul breath of persistent vice, or by the secret plotting of shameless disorder and disloyalty. The harmless pranks of frolicsome youth can be generously borne with if they are accompanied by the honor and manliness which cannot endure the slightest shadow of falsehood or deception; but let every parent be assured that in this school his son or daughter shall not be tempted by the presence of tobacco and gum-soaked, lewd, lying, thieving, perversely mischievous or recklessly lazy companions.

This is a Christian school. Such may it ever remain. Sooner than it shall dishonor the name it bears, and deny the faith of its founders, and join the ranks of blank agnosticism and foul misbelief, may the elements crumble its walls to the earth, and oblivion hide its name from the memory of man.[87]

* * *

I should not like to ask the academy freshman about the importance of the study of Latin. I remember . . . the time when I began Latin. I would not have been fit to pass on the question. No academy freshman is. But I would not hesitate to ask any of the college students as to the value of the study of Latin . . . .

I am certain that if we catch the real purpose of a college education, we will have no question as to the place of these studies in our curriculum.[88]

* * *

Plutarch says, "The essential things in the education of the young are to teach them to worship, to revere their parents, to honor their elders, to obey the laws, to submit to rulers, to love their friends, to be temperate." These essential things Plutarch mentioned seem to be the only subjects omitted in the modern textbooks . . . . If a student does not learn them somewhere he will never amount to much.

God called Abraham out from his home, and his years of rigid discipline gave him the essential training that made it possible for him to stand as the head of a mighty race with great promise. This race, in time, was called out and disciplined by forty years of wilderness tribulation, during which time they learned the value of government . . . . "He did what was right in his own eyes" is just another way of saying he did wrong . . . . When Christ came to Israel and displayed so much power, they were angered because He would not lead them in revolt against the ruling authorities, but they were wholly unfitted to enjoy the blessings of independence. He showed by His life, His example, His teaching that He believed in authority and in respecting authority . . . .

We are again in this age confronted with the problem of submission to authority . . . the recognition of authority. . . .

Education that lacks discipline lacks its right leg. A college that is above discipline is below wisdom. Of all the ignorance in the world the greatest is that which lets a student do as he pleases, e.g. that which lets an undergraduate choose the courses that are supposed to educate him. If he could choose them, he would need no education. Letting a boy have his own way merely to keep him quiet and satisfied is like giving a baby an open razor for the same purpose.[89]

Of this lecture from which the above excerpt is taken, a student commented in the *Journal*:

At the regular chapel hour on December 14, J. D. Charles delivered a lecture on "The Educational and Cultural Value of Government and Discipline." Professor Charles spoke almost an hour and was completely master of his subject at every moment he was on the floor. He had his subject well outlined and prepared, and as he proceeded in his characteristic manner, every listener was fully absorbed in his clear exposition and logical argument. Immediately after the address, calls came for its publication in pamphlet form. Excerpts of the address will be printed in later issues of the *Journal*.[90]

Alta Mae Eby in a term address counseled students that in choosing a course

one should eliminate a narrow self-interest which can see only that side of a question which has for the individual a practical significance. The most practical side of education most of us do not recognize . . . . One of our greatest needs is power. This we get through power-training subjects—Latin, algebra, geography, history. Surely those were wise men who first placed these subjects in the curriculum; and just because we cannot see their practical value is no reason we should not take them.[91]

Edward Yoder, as an academy graduate, gave a commencement speech on "The Uses of Adversity." An excerpt follows:

The formulators of our modern educational ideals seem almost to have lost sight of some of the uses of adversity.

> Their aim is to remove from the child's path all possible difficulties and obstacles. Orison Swett Marden says in this connection: "This is the crutch age. 'Helps' and 'Aids' are advertised everywhere. Our thinking is done for us in 'explanations' and 'keys'. 'Short roads' and 'abridged methods' are characteristic of the century. Newspapers give us our politics and preachers our religion."
>
> Might it be possible that some of our educational methods are defeating the very end toward which we profess to be working? Could it furthermore be possible that we are depriving the learner of the very things which he needs for the development of the highest type of character?[92]

These educators made a valiant fight for hard work. Because they recognized that progress in the future could be built only on the cultural heritages of the past, they labored zealously to lead students deep into the fonts of knowledge. Whether they were right or wrong, their principles have produced men and women of sturdy, far-seeing character who have in our generation been assigned leadership in many of our church boards and institutions.

The financial struggle through these years was a cautious but not a strenuous one. Work on the Administration Building had begun in 1914. An agreement had been made with the contractor that construction should cease each time funds were exhausted.[93] ". . . for we had made a ruling that the institution should not go into debt for another building."[94] After the foundation was finished in 1915, work on the building did cease for a year. On March 21, 1916, the bricklaying began with F. G. Roupp as general contractor, Ezra King in charge of the concrete work, and J. C. Reynolds of Valley Center, Kansas, in charge of bricklaying.[95]

By June, 1916, the walls were complete, and in the roofless chapel hall all commencement programs were held. During the summer the roof was put on; and after the wiring, plumb-

With the addition of the Administration Building, the school became "Hesston College and Bible School" in 1918-1919.

ing, and plastering were done, funds were again exhausted. The alumni at the spring meeting had pledged $5,000. The solicitor, L. O. King, before starting on his tour, conducted chapel and called for a pledge of $1,000 from the school itself. In fifteen minutes teachers and students had subscribed more than $1,200. In February, 1917, came another lull; rooms were yet unfinished. The contractor took a job in a Wichita car factory. T. M. Erb wrote, "We cannot finish the new college building."[96] By May, 1918, they "lacked $1,000-1,500 to pay for a heating plant."[97] In response to an appeal "One brother gave $1,000 and promised $1,000 as a loan without interest."[98]

By August, 1918, the building was ready with "the large skylight in the library, . . . rolling partitions separating the assembly hall proper from the Y.P.C.A. room in the rear, and the Alumni Room up the stairway opposite the library door."[99]

The business manager was the first to move into the new building on August 24, 1918.[100] The dedication program for the Administration Building was held on January 2, 1919.

9:30 a.m.
Devotional
History and Purpose of Hesston College and Bible School
—President D. H. Bender
Music   Ladies' Chorus
Dedicatory Sermon   Daniel Kauffman
Financial Report   T. M. Erb

Evening Session—7:30 p.m.
Music   Men's Chorus
Religious Standards of Our Schools   Daniel Kauffman
Christian Education   J. E. Hartzler
What the Church Expects of Her Schools   S. C. Yoder
Relation of the General Board to the Colleges
D. G. Lapp
Music   Ladies' Chorus[101]

Two months after the dedication this declaration appeared in the *Journal*:

The new building is completed and paid for. Now we are planning the new dormitory that is a part of the original plan of the founders . . . the same distance south of the pavilion as the other dormitory is north. Subscriptions are already coming in.[102]

While the Administration Building was being constructed, other campus improvements were kept at a minimum. Each year more trees were planted. Another well was added and a few repairs were made.

In 1919-20, only a year after the dedication of the new building, the president wrote, "Our fond hope is that in another year we may realize the benefits of our new dormitory."[103]

By April the new dormitory fund had grown

to over $3,000, all without any special solicitation. The building will be U style, with the closed part of the U facing north toward the other dorm . . . . The building will be named "Hess Hall."[104]

In September, 1920, construction began—excavating, sand and cement hauling. By April, foundations were being put in. Six years later in a little pamphlet entitled, "Our Financial Story," the president wrote:

> The work of excavation began in the fall of 1920. Having completed the basement walls, we found ourselves in the financial slump following the war, and since no indebtedness-for-buildings was our slogan, work on the new dorm ceased. It is, however, our intention to complete this building as soon as financial conditions warrant.

The 1927-28 catalog expressed a waning hope.

> This building was to be a second dormitory—for girls . . . . Recently there has been a move made to use this foundation upon which to erect a much needed auditorium.

Although the dormitory fund failed to grow, other campus developments had sprung up roundabout. In 1920-21 the students had decided

> to take matters into their own hands and raise enough money to erect some type of temporary building which would answer the purpose of a gymnasium until a permanent structure could be put up by the school.[105]

The athletic association consulted the local board, which pledged full moral support, but none financially. The board, moreover, limited the solicitation of funds to alumni, ex-students, and businessmen of the town.

The drive was on. The idea was conceived in September; by October 14, students had collected $407 in the out-of-school group. The same day they staged a chapel drive with Joseph Graber, chairman; Willard Smith to present "Needs;" Alvin King, "Plans;" and Paul Erb, "Figures." To start building, $700 in cash was needed. The chairman called for $300 from the student body, which added to the $407 already in hand, assured immediate action. Before chapel ended, the total rose to $1,350; and the building forthwith began with Roy King, a student, as foreman, and plans to complete the construction in four weeks. The students donated the labor. Six weeks later it was finished and dedicated with ceremony highlighted by an oration by Joseph Graber "On the Passing of the Old Gymnasium," the Exercise Shed other students had built back in 1913.

Academy freshman basketball team, 1925. E. Flaming, physical education director.

In the same year the school bought the laundry which M. E. Hostetler had earlier built on the campus west of Green Gables, and granted him permission to build a home on the campus, a house purchased by the institution later for a Home Economics Cottage. Since 1948, it is being used as a private home. It was during this same time that J. L. Shellenberger, the farm manager, leased a plot of ground on which to build a home for his family, a house which was the "College Farm Home" until 1956-57, when it became a boys' rooming house.

The Audubon Society was organized in 1920-21 and began

erecting birdhouses and feeding stations. Under the vigorous direction of Esther Good, the dean of women, lilac bushes, tulips, hyacinths, and canna lilies were planted near the dormitory. Trees were dug up on Iowa and Missouri farms and sent in by ex-students and friends—Jacob Erb, L. J. Miller, S. B. Miller, Myron Yoder, Chris Graber. South of the Administration Building was an "Iowa Grove" of oak, elm, hickory, and maple trees, planted and replanted for a number of years. The school purchased ten acres west of the buildings to add to the campus. Anna F. Byler in her will left the college a gift of nearly $1,000. Student mail was for the first time placed in individual boxes "on the counter in the business manager's office."

The HESSTON COLLEGE JOURNAL staff, 1919-1920. Standing, left to right: S. M. King '19, '23; J. D. Graber '22; Phebe Ann King '22; Paul Bender '16, '21; Paul Erb '14. Seated: Edward Yoder '17, '20 and Anna Loucks '22.

From 1920-21 until after the depression years, the pillar that went before seemed to become indistinct, to stand still and bid them wait. The founders one by one were taken away. Material improvements after that time were minor ones, chiefly class gifts—a slide projector, bulletin board, drinking fountain, lockers and showers—in Green Gables for the girls and in the basement of the Administration Building for the boys.

Although there was little advancement in campus construction during the late twenties, the institution kept itself on a secure financial footing.

> Except for the first year, the school was able for ten years to keep its operating expenses within the operating income. During this time after balancing our accounts we found ourselves ahead on a few occasions, but after putting in the College Department we began to run behind until by 1925 we had accumulated a total deficit of about $8,000. To wipe out this indebtedness, the third drive was instituted. We received in cash and pledges just a little more than $10,000. Thus the school is again out of debt and can look the world squarely in the face.[106]

After 1926 until 1930, the end of the Bender administration, graduating classes gave the sundial and lawn benches and began work on the Bird Sanctuary plans.

Two business developments of the period are noteworthy. From the beginning, alumni had been interested in an endowment fund for the College. To build up this fund, each alumnus was assessed $1 annually. By 1923, the total amount given by alumni was $1,200. Annual fees were then discontinued, expenses met by luncheon fees, and endowment money accumulated by donations. From 1924-26, alumni swelled their fund to $2,000, another $1,000 came from outside alumni ranks, and the 1924 class made their gift a donation to the fund. The sum of $20,000 was the full junior college standardization requirement and the goal set for Hesston College by the Mennonite Board of Education in a church-wide endowment program drive launched in 1927 and approved by the confer-

ences.[107] By January 1, 1927, two men—Abram Eby of Lyman,
Mississippi, and D. S. Weaver of La Junta, Colorado—with a
gift of $16,000 swelled the $3,000 on hand "to almost $20,000
with an annual interest of almost $1,000.[108] The goal for Hess-
ton College in a three-year endowment program the Board was
then promoting was $60,000. To aid in the campaign of the
Board the alumni then began a vigorous drive "to raise $10,000
in the next three years."[109] Within the first year they collected
$4,096.90, "leaving $5,903.10 to be raised in the next two
years." The city of Hesston added $4,000, and a *Journal* writer
figured, "now we have one-half of the $60,000."[110]

During the same time, the finance committee of the Mennonite Board of Education had in hand a resolution of the local
board of Hesston College:

> Resolved that in interpreting the mind of A. L. Hess in
> donating the farm on which Hesston College and Bible
> School is located it is our opinion that this farm should be
> held for the Mennonite Board of Education by a Board of
> Trustees at Hesston and the income applied to Hesston
> College as an Endowment Income. Done in regular session at
> Hesston, May 15, 1928.

The Mennonite Board of Education voted that the executive
committee of the board "negotiate with the A. L. Hess trustees
for a deed of transfer to the Mennonite Board of Education of
the Hesston College and Bible School campus and buildings."[111]

The new catalog issued in the spring of 1930 stated that

> approximately $40,000 has been paid and pledged as
> endowment for Hesston College and Bible School . . .
> up to this time. . . . Including the invested funds which
> are already producing income, the total productive endow-
> ment is around $60,000.[112]

Student expenses rose gradually during the period. In 1915-
16, as at the beginning, tuition was $45 per year for academy
students; for college students it was $54. Board was $104 per

year. By 1930, academy tuition had become $65 per year; college tuition $100, and board $140.

Teachers' salaries rose even less substantially during the twenty-one years. The president's annual salary by 1916-17, the term when two years of college were first given, had risen from $720 to $820; J. D. Charles' from $60 per month to $780 per year; T. M. Erb from $25 per month to $460 per year. Alta Mae Eby was receiving $560 and M. D. Landis $485. By 1920 the president received $1,300 annually and the dean $1,250—the highest salary J. D. Charles received during his services at Hesston. D. H. Bender's salary never rose above $1,350. The early leaders frequently stated that salaries must be kept on a mission basis.

During these first twenty-one years there occurred numerous incidents of dramatic significance at the time. The hall manager, Noah Oyer, surprised faculty and students by marrying the matron, Siddie King, soon after his graduation. As a student, Paul Erb admired one of his teachers and married her as soon as he too became a teacher. A fire broke out in the Hesston Hotel and within an hour burned down the restaurant, post office, and barbershop. Students were on hand in night array. One brave student rushed into the burning building, whisked a huge bevelled mirror from the wall, ran across the street with it and flung it on a pile of furniture where it crashed into a dozen pieces. Unaware of any mishap—he dashed back for more. In 1923 the chorus delivered May baskets up and down the town and stopped in the center of Main Street to sing "The Hallelujah Chorus." Once "Jerky," the Hesston train, got stuck in a snowdrift just outside Hesston and the "academy boys helped shovel her out." In 1918-19, school was closed for a month by order of Governor Capper because of the influenza epidemic. That year there was no Christmas vacation except on Christmas Day and New Year; and throughout the spring, school was held each Saturday until 12:30. Oft-requested music numbers were "Backbone" by the Men's Chorus, a duet—"David and Jonathan"—by M. D. Landis and Paul Erb, and the "Sextet from 'Lucia,' " in which J. D. Charles sang. Vachel Lindsay, "the tramp poet," chanted his poetry at the college on February 26, 1929. In 1922 at the close of school the Missouri-Pacific Railway sent a special coach from Kansas City to take students to their homes. A representative of the company came to the college to sell tickets and check baggage. In 1925-26 Paul W. Miller of Idaho painted the sign, "Welcome to Green Gables;" in January, 1919, the first electric washing machines were installed in the college laundry; and on October 7, 1929, the first electric refrigerator was brought to the college kitchen. On October 25, 1927, the Administration Building traffic rules still in practice were devised by Ida Hostetler Sommerfeld.

There were grave events too. The First World War came, and the Mennonite Church had to clarify its relationship to the government. Boys who stood firm on nonparticipation in war were isolated, ridiculed, and mistreated in military camps. Mennonite leaders near-by were misunderstood and were "tarred and feathered." In recording the happening in his diary, T. M. Erb wrote, "O God, help us to be true, and forgive the perpetrators."[113] Of the ten students who had gone into Near East Relief Service, Menno Shellenberger died there. In 1916-17 Oakley Wenger died during the school year, "the first among the student body and faculty in the history of the school." Then came the deaths of A. L. Hess in 1920, of J. D. Charles in 1923, and of T. M. Erb in 1929, and the resignation of D. H. Bender in 1930.

Time had taken its toll, tasks begun were left unfinished, the financial depression grew more and more severe, and a fog settled down over the institution.

> *But if the cloud were not taken up, then they journeyed not till the day that it was taken up.*
>
> —Exodus 40:37

IV. TWO YEARS WITHOUT A PRESIDENT, 1930-1932

*And when the cloud tarried long upon the taber-
nacle many days, then they kept the charge of the
Lord, and journeyed not.* —Numbers 9:19

D. H. Bender resigned in the summer of 1930. Until a new
president could be chosen, the Mennonite Board of Education

Edward Yoder, third dean, 1924-1932; and chairman of the
administrative committee, 1930-1932.

appointed an administrative committee of four members to
direct the institution—Edward Yoder, dean; I. E. Burkhart,
head of the Bible Department; Paul Erb, registrar; and Maurice

97

A. Yoder, business manager. Edward Yoder was appointed chairman of the committee, "assuming all duties usually devolving upon the president, in addition to the regular duties of chairman of such a committee."[1] A study committee was also appointed to investigate the local and church-wide problems relating to Hesston College before a reorganization should be attempted.

As a result of the financial depression and repeated crop failures in the West, the enrollment had been gradually decreasing since 1927. In 1930-31, the year the committee took charge, there was another decided reduction. In 1927-28 the enrollment had reached 248; in 1930-31, it was 148 including spring term and correspondence students. As early as September 12, 1930, the local board, whose charter members—with the exception of C. M. Hostetler—had by this time all been replaced by new personnel,[2] was discussing ways of meeting a probable deficit of $10,000 "instead of $4,000 as per budget, brought about by the decreased enrollment." As the year progressed, the financial situation grew critical. The business manager made frequent appeals to the Board of Education for help, did solicitation in neighboring states as early as November, and made strong and continuous efforts to collect long-standing accounts and encourage prompt settlement of new ones. Companies were constantly demanding payment and there was nothing in the college treasury with which to satisfy them. One breath of relief was a $500 gift for running expenses from Mr. Joliffe, a banker in Peabody.

In spite of financial difficulties the administration and the faculty were alert and active. New trends were evident in the curriculum. A strong junior college consciousness was astir. The dean wrote:

The junior college is the newest unit in the American educational system. Within a third of a century almost five hundred institutions of this class have come into being and the idea is rapidly spreading. Being new, this unit is less traditionalized and more rapidly adapted to actual needs than is the older college organization.

The junior colleges have not deliberately sawed off and appropriated the first two years of the college course. Their curricula represent natural units, separated from what is above them in methods of study and teaching. The junior college years are more closely related to the high school than to the senior college, for they are generally considered now as the completion of secondary education.

The junior college offers in its education courses a preparation for elementary school teaching. It offers in its foundation courses and in its training in tool knowledges a splendid preparation for a senior college course, or for entrance to professional schools.[3]

In consequence of this new movement, there was a decided shift toward practical, vocational courses. Normal training was taken out of the academy curriculum and increased emphasis put upon it in college. Students did practice teaching in the Hesston Grade School and in rural schools in the community. By January 13 the faculty discussed "The Feasibility of Adding Home Economics or Manual Training to the Curriculum." The administrative committee added a course in drawing the second semester of 1930-31,[4] and sewing and voice classes the next year.[5] There were college and academy public speaking classes. The aim of the four-year Bible course, as stated in the 1931 *Lark*, "is especially intended to give practical training for Y.P.C.A. activities, Sunday School and home and foreign mission work, daily vacation and week day Bible Schools, and Gospel Ministry."

There were other evidences of faculty alertness. A strong study crusade was in progress. Mrs. Erb gave annual rousing study talks in chapel, and a committee was appointed to formu-

late and administer an extensive questionnaire to aid students
in the development of effective study habits. Physical examinations for students and physical training were incorporated in-

Administrative Committee, 1930-1932. Left to right: Edward
Yoder '17, '20, dean and chairman of committee; I. E. Burkhart
'22, '25, head of the Bible Department; Paul Erb '14, registrar
and secretary of committee; and Maurice A. Yoder '23, '25,
business manager.

to the school program. The peace committee prepared an
Armistice Day program. The second spring term, "especially
for rural teachers," was held. There were discussions about
differences between college and academy students, the significance of such differences, and the necessity of giving individual
attention to students requiring it. The most extensive extracurricular activity of the administration during that year was
an effort to bolster the faith of the constituency in the school
and to encourage continued support. As the financial panic
grew more severe and the finances of the school more critical,
rumors that the school would be closed were occasionally set
afloat. The administrative committee soon after its appointment sent out letters to the churches assuring them that the
school would continue as usual. The committee made an appeal to the Board of Education for an early appointment of a
president. A faculty committee sent out a questionnaire to
alumni, ex-students, and church leaders asking if they con-

sidered the work of Hesston College worthwhile. Encouraging responses were published and circulated. The reply from Noah Oyer, then dean of Goshen College, is particularly noteworthy:

> The test (of a school) after all lies in the ability of the student to go out and transmit something of what he absorbed in his college days.
>
> How does Hesston College measure up to this test? I was interested in this question last summer while studying in the library of one of our eastern universities. Surrounding me were catalogues from almost all the colleges and universities in the United States. I went to the alcove where the Hesston Catalogue was located and looked over the list of alumni members recorded in the last pages of the book.
>
> To one who has been rather intimately acquainted with the institution from the second year of its history to the present time, a perusal of the list brought back many pleasant memories. But the thing that impressed me most in those moments I stole from my regular studies, was the academic-mindedness of the college graduates. I found that two-thirds of those who had been graduated from Hesston College with the Bachelor of Arts degree have continued their studies in the graduate school. A large number of these have completed one year of work leading to the Master's degree. Three of them have continued their studies to the completion of the Ph.D. degree. The interest of others took them into the Theological Seminary. All of them, including those who did not pursue their studies further than the undergraduate college, are filling worthy places in life.[6]

During the year, 1930-31, Noah Oyer, one of the most kindly, solicitous builders of Hesston College, died. In the memorial service held at Hesston College Edward Yoder, the dean who had succeeded him at Hesston, gave him this tribute:

> The pioneers did with their might what their hands found to do. Brother Oyer, who even before his graduation from college had decided to accept the invitation to labor in the school and in particular to prepare himself as its Bible teacher, already at that time saw the vision of Hesston College and Bible School giving thorough instruction in approved and accredited courses. His vision included, along with the best educational standards, a distinctly evangelical, Biblical, and denominational emphasis.[7]

His obituary ended with this tribute: "His character was marked by simplicity, modesty, refinement, as well as unusual wisdom and insight."[8]

Student activities, like those of the faculty, were alive and vigorous during these two years. The athletic association recommended that the gymnasium "be rented . . . to the Phillips 66 Team two evenings a week . . . and to the Grade School boys on Saturday . . . provided it does not in any way conflict with its use by the school, nor interfere with study or public meetings, and that the campus and school property be properly taken care of, and that no matched games of outside teams be played on the campus."[9] The clubs organized by the faculty in the previous year had died; and the literary societies were revived, three in the academy—Philomathean, Victorian, and Excelsior—and one in the college, the Bryan-Delphian, a combination of the two previous ones. A German Society, Der Triumphierende Verein, was active for a number of years. The public programs given by the groups gave evidence of the general curricular swing toward the current and the practical. One program was a court trial with Sara Flisher and Gideon G. Yoder as the attorneys and one consisted entirely of the reading of recent poetry. Others were traditional—essay contests, debates, and informative speeches.

Before the year came to a close the Board of Education at its annual meeting passed a motion "that Hesston College and Bible School be authorized to continue its program for 1931-32, and that its work be continued in the hands of the present administrative committee."[10] In the second year, 1931-32, the enrollment dropped to 70, "the lowest since more than ten years ago." State accreditment was withdrawn,[11] and the Board of Education met to consider closing the school.[12] An analysis of the replies to the questionnaire sent out the previous year indicated that the alumni almost unanimously thought it unwise to close the school, that they wanted both the academy and the college, that they did not want the institution to be only a Bible School, that they did favor the strengthening of the present Bible curriculum, and that they strongly approved the addition of vocational courses. The attributes they thought most important in a president of Hesston College were education, the quality to maintain the confidence of the church, spirituality, doctrinal soundness, executive ability, and ability to win the confidence of young people. The order in which the items are listed shows which received the greater number of votes. Other qualities receiving fewer votes were sociability, personality, financial judgment, leadership, broadmindedness, experience, and tact.[13]

On October 20, 1931, the executive committee of the Board of Education, the executive committee of the Missouri-Kansas Conference, the local board and faculty of Hesston College, and numerous other church leaders held a meeting at the Pennsylvania Church near Hesston to consider the problems of the school. "All bore united testimony to the providential guidance of the school in the past, to the immeasurable service the school has rendered to the Church, and to the need of continuing the work if at all possible."[14]

The recommendations adopted at the meeting were
> that the school should be continued, that financial problems should be met with the utmost conservatism within the school and with the cooperation of the constituency, and that the organization and program for 1932-33 be made within our means and prospects.[15]

A bishop from Colorado wrote, "True we are suffering from a financial depression, but if a constituency of less than one-half as many as ours had the faith 23 years ago to start at the bottom and work up to the present, why should we lose heart? While we may not be able to meet certain standards in the educational world, we can do our best to meet the needs of our own people."[16]

Immediately after the decision to continue "within our means and prospects," the administration began an onslaught to cut the budget and meet operating expenses and ultimately to save the school. A parent-teachers meeting was held to find a common ground and to promote understanding and cooperation. Statements of "Personal Benefits Received at Hesston College" were printed and circulated. Letters were sent to the executive committee of the Missouri-Kansas Conference about raising money for the deficit of Hesston College. The college employed a student to bake bread, discontinued the school laundry, decided to publish the *Journal* bi-monthly, and in personal consultation with Dean Yoder the faculty volunteered to reduce their salaries all the way from $9\frac{1}{2}$ to $35\frac{1}{2}$ per cent. The average reduction was 29 per cent. Even then, by May 10, teachers' salaries were two and one-half months in arrears; and bills due to business houses amounted to $1134. The net operating deficit in 1930-31 had been $6,073, and in 1931-32 it was $12,618.

By March, 1932, the *Journal* announced that the junior college would be suspended for the year 1932-33; and by May 10, the community proposed to the local board that the academy department be operated as an accredited high school under the Barnes Law of Kansas.[17]

But, at last the cloud seemed to be lifting. On April 2, 1932, the executive committee of the Mennonite Board of Education in consultation with representative groups and leaders in the West, appointed Milo Kauffman as the new president of Hesston College and received a practically unanimous approval of the appointment. The president-elect had been connected with the school since 1919 and had wide experience as an evangelist and as a worker with young people. He had spent three years of study in Chicago, where he had received a B. D. degree from Northern Baptist Theological Seminary and an M. A. degree from the McCormick Theological Seminary. Almost immediately after his appointment he came to Hesston College to study its possibilities and limitations and to begin reorganization.

V. THE KAUFFMAN ADMINISTRATION, 1932-1951

*And when the cloud tarried long . . . many days,
then (they) kept the charge of the Lord, and journeyed not.*

*. . . according to the commandment of the Lord they
abode in their tents, and according to the commandment of the Lord they journeyed.*

—Numbers 9:19, 20

A RE-BEGINNING, 1932-33

The situation into which the new president came was not a
promising one. The enrollment had dwindled to 50; there
were five teachers, each promised a salary of $35 per month
"provided it does not exceed the income of the year." When
the first year began, the girls were all moved to first floor of
Green Gables, the boys to second floor, and third was "left to
the cobwebs." The general and local boards had considered
closing the Administration Building and holding classes in the
dormitory but decided the idea was "neither economical nor
advisable." The college owed money to business houses and
creditors were urging payment, teachers weren't being paid,[1]
and the deficit was looming. The Mennonite Board of Education had "moved that Hesston College suspend its College
department for 1932-33."[2] The Board reported, "Burdens both
spiritual and financial appear to be grave, and the responsibility
of carrying on interests involved is more than can be borne
without the aid of Divine Wisdom."[3]

The new president, while attending seminary and engaging
widely in evangelistic work, was cautioned by friends against

106

Milo Kauffman, second president of Hesston College, 1932-1951.

identifying himself with "a dying cause." In a confidence that upheld him through the difficult years, he replied with conviction, "Hesston College is the Lord's work. I am not only willing to identify myself with it, but I'm willing to attempt to lead it out of its difficulty. And if it must die, I am willing to die with it."[4] During the second month of school he wrote to the Mennonite Board of Education:

> The amount given some of these teachers is not enough to keep them going. The rent, interest, and taxes some have to pay consumes almost the entire amount . . . . I am planning on getting enough out of evangelistic work so that I will need to

107

draw only $15 per month to get the same as the others. In fact, I hope that some months I will not have to draw from the school at all, but let it go on the allowances of the other faculty members.

In the salary schedule set up by the local board the new president's allowance was listed $15 per month.

To relieve the hard-pressed financial situation Paul Erb, secretary of the business committee, wrote letters of appeal to ex-students with unpaid bills; the Missouri-Kansas and the Iowa-Nebraska conferences were appealed to for cooperation in meeting the 1931-32 deficit; and the executive committee of the Board of Education was urged "to continue its efforts to raise the amount it has assumed for Hesston College and Bible School."[5] To the appeal the Iowa-Nebraska Conference responded:

In regard to the present deficit of the last school year of Hesston College and Bible School, we commission the School Committee to work a plan for securing the further cooperation of the members of this district in meeting this deficit and we urge that in as far as possible from henceforth the school should be operated within her income.[6]

Although the hard-pressed congregations did not "meet the quota assigned to them"[7] there were many sympathizing "donors of supplies to the faculty."[8] The Harper, Kansas congregation sent "a load of provisions;" Milford, Nebraska, sent 200 bushels of corn for the farm; Chris Vogt and H. A. Diener each gave a cow to the college dairy; and some farmers paid their bills with wheat.

To encourage an increase in enrollment the local board voted a "reduction of 30% in student expenses." Tuition was $25 per semester, room $16-18, and board $50. The children of ministers, missionaries, and faculty members received 50% reductions; and there were no tuition charges for Bible subjects.

During the new president's first year, 1932-33, the cloud

seemed to be lifting—very, very slowly. The total enrollment including Special Bible Term students was 125 compared with 105 of the previous year. The Special Bible Term enrollment was 56, "the second highest in the history of the school."[9] In February the president was able to report to the Board, "during the current year, the 1931-32 deficit has been reduced about $1000. The school is operating this year on its income. Plans next year are to reduce students' expenses and to do considerable solicitation."[10] He thanked the Missouri-Kansas and Iowa-Nebraska Conferences for their "interest and cooperation in meeting the 1931-32 deficit of Hesston College." And again he appealed to the Board "to cooperate with the Hesston College Administration in a liquidation of the remainder of the debt."[11]

Although materially the school was at a mid-depression standstill, the five underpaid teachers—President Milo Kauffman, Dean Paul Erb, I. E. Burkhart, D. D. Driver, and Alta Housour—strove to keep alive a buoyant spirit and a high grade of scholarship. A strong evangelism emphasis was evident; and in keeping with the trend of the times, a strong steady shift from the classical to the practical continued. The junior college was not accredited; but the school gave courses to the eight college students who came, and Goshen College accepted the credits. Mrs. Erb continued giving her pointed study talks in which she convinced students that blaming unprepared lessons on teachers, on long or difficult assignments, on a confusion of circumstances, or on a lack of native ability was merely transparent rationalizing. In graphic, step-by-step instruction she showed students how to prevent mind-wandering, how to master assignments, how to plan and to use study schedules, and how to develop and sustain strong study habits.[12]

To quicken interest in extracurricular activities, the faculty

suggested a variety of clubs to replace the literary societies—
Science Club, Junior Homemakers, Mennonite Historical Society, Travel Club, Art Club, and the Audubon Society. The
Mennonite Historical Society had been active for two years
in 1923-25. It was revived in 1930, continuing only to 1933.[13]
Its membership list is impressive, heavy with names well-known
in the Mennonite Church. The Y in its drive raised $117.57;
Men's and Ladies' Choruses and the *Lark* and *Journal* staffs
functioned as usual.

As an economy effort that first year a printing press donated
by Jess Kauffman, a student, was installed in the basement of
the Administration Building to print report cards and letter-
heads.

Two noteworthy happenings occurred during the year. Since
1919 the foundation for a proposed girls' dormitory had
disfigured the campus. General Conference was scheduled to
meet in Hesston in the summer of 1933. On January 10, 1933,
the local board "favored the removal of the old foundation."
The Board of Education in its February, 1933 notes included a
recommendation from the executive committee "that the basement wall on the Hesston College campus be razed." A. N.
Troyer, the acting business manager, had charge of removing
the foundation. On March 20, 1933, with donated help from
the city and township and from the Hesston, Pennsylvania, and
Spring Valley (Canton) congregations, the foundation was
razed, the site leveled, and the materials hauled away with no
expense to the college. The evergreens and spirea around
the foundation were sold to pay for the blasting.[14]

Another happening of the year was a tragic one, reminiscent
of one previously reported in this history. Maurice A. Yoder,
assistant pastor of the congregation and a faculty member who
was not, however, serving during the year, had set up a shop

Maurice A. Yoder.

in his garage. On March 6, a blowtorch set afire his clothing and the garage. He was so seriously burned that his leg had to be amputated. Although seven years later his other leg also needed to be removed, he is still (in 1959) a full-time instructor, walks to school, drives his own car, and occasionally

111

travels quite extensively for ministerial or for professional reasons.

The first year of the new administration the cloud "tarried and they journeyed not." But there was evidence that those in charge were aware that the cloud was hovering over them and that sometime again it would go before and begin its forward movement. They were biding their time. "At the commandment of the Lord" they would begin their forward march.

UPGRADE, 1933-1938

The first six years of the new administration were a slow painstaking ascent out of depression. The program had to be gaged to severely limited finances. The administration was annually reminded to "operate within income."

In 1934-35 Amos Gingerich became business manager. His thrifty, conservative policies are evident in the reports of those years. He added his own Guernseys to the college dairy herd; he planned to supply all the meat for the college dining room from the college farm; he had the electric refrigerator turned off during the winter and gave constant reminders to economize on water and light bills.

Throughout these strenuous upgrade years he carried on a constructive repair program. In 1936-37 gas was installed in the furnaces and the kitchen stove. New flexatile flooring was laid in the entrance to the Administration Building and hardwood floors in Green Gables. The buildings were repainted. The Hostetler house on the campus was turned into a home economics cottage. A campus improvement committee was appointed, the campus was landscaped, and a new improvement plan launched. New sidewalks were built; a grove of Austrian pines was planted north of the dormitory, and shrubs and trees around the buildings; and the trees along the half moon were realigned.[15]

In a report to the Board of Education on May 20, 1937, the treasurer of the board stated that enrollments had increased in the last three years, that the schools were operating within budgets and "without deficits the past five years," buildings and equipment were being improved, and standing debts were being reduced.[16]

Enrollments climbed gradually during these six years. In 1932-33 there were 55 regular students and 56 in Special Bible Term; in 1933-34, 98 regular and 71 in Special Term; by 1937-38 the figures had climbed to 177 regular and 100 Special Term students. During these six years the Special Bible Term enrollment annually broke previous records.[17] With the enrollments rose faculty salaries from $30 in 1932-33 to $50 in 1934-35. By 1937-38 the highest salaries had reached $90 per month.[18]

By 1935 the administrative lines had become well-drawn. Assisting the president were Paul Erb, the dean and librarian, and D. D. Driver, registrar. To support these officials an administrative cabinet was organized to direct and report various school activities.[19]

As director of publicity and publications in the new cabinet organization, the president as early as 1935 began to urge more advertising, more visiting of churches, the publishing of more bulletins. By 1936 with the help of the Board of Education, he had devised a plan for a thorough canvass of the entire constituency to raise funds for reducing the debt incurred prior to 1932. Many weeks of the winter and practically all the summer months the president spent soliciting among the churches. In 1935-36 he appealed to the general board for a half-time field man. The Board responded by appointing the president himself to serve as field man, as the college solicitor.[20] He was already carrying a full teaching load—church history, evangelism, child study, inspirational hour, and psychology[21]—acting as director of publicity and publications and director of discipline on the newly organized cabinet, directing annually a number of evangelistic meetings and serving the home congregation as pastor.

The president began his new task with vigor. The dean had consulted state authorities about re-accreditation for the junior college. They informed him that the greatest aid in securing state accreditment was more substantial financial support by the constituency. The library, laboratories, and classrooms needed standard equipment, and teachers needed more substantial allowances to encourage additional training. In his report to the cabinet the dean said, "State authorities will be impressed with deeds, not promises."[22]

The new field man began activities at home first. With the businessmen of the city he organized a community drive. Slogans—"Help The College Regain Its State Accreditment"— were posted in the windows of business houses and later a dinner of appreciation was served to the businessmen of the community. The faculty entertained the grade school teachers and the county superintendent. A parent-teachers' meeting was organized and carried on for several years. The Kansas alumni were organized into fellowship groups "to foster fellowship, to disseminate information, to unify efforts, to secure funds, ultimately to secure state accreditment for the junior college."[23] Solicitation in the churches west of the Mississippi River was intensified.

Within the institution, advance strides were also being made. A system of scholarships was planned, in 1937 the academy department rating was again raised from C to A, and by the opening of the next school year, 1938-39, the junior college department was re-accredited by the state. Added evidence of an imminent forward move by the tarrying cloud was local board authorization to purchase the Cooprider or Cassler properties for dormitory use, in case the purchase could be arranged without financial obligation to the board.[24]

Matching the efforts of the president were those of the dean. Paul Erb served as dean and librarian, taught a full load— English IV, English composition, college public speaking, life of Christ, music II, theory of music—was director of men's and ladies' choruses and the all-school chorus, and served as pastor of the Pennsylvania congregation.[25] An admiring student wrote in the school *Journal,* "Put what you call a dry subject into his schedule and floods shall cover the desert."[26] During the six climbing-back years, Erb was constantly adjusting the curriculum to new trends. New courses were added in manual training, home economics, business, modern languages. When no modern language teacher was immediately available, he planned that students needing the courses could take them by tutoring arrangements at Bethel College. He visited classes and counseled teachers. Monthly round-table discussions on professional and informative subjects were held in faculty meetings on topics like "Events in Germany and Their Relation to World Events," "Building Student Morale," "Study of the Adolescent," "The Expression of Aesthetic Impulses," "The Project Method." Every teacher was asked each year to give an informative or inspirational speech in chapel. In March, 1936, as librarian, the dean reported to the Cabinet that during that year there had been "more investment in the library than in any year since 1929," that the library workers were cataloguing pictures and bibliographies and building up pamphlet files, and that new books, more magazines, and a

1936 revision of the *Encyclopedia Americana* were added.

The dean was alert, resourceful, and experimentative. In 1936 two-hour periods were tried for academy classes. Scholarship tests were given to all students. All English classes worked out, under careful guidance, prepared exercises combining art appreciation and the use of the library during National Art Week, while Mrs. Erb organized and supervised a rotating art exhibit. The dean had many of the more famous paintings with illuminative comments posted in conspicuous places in the halls and classrooms. There were frequent talks in chapel on events and issues of the day. The dean wrote letters to the parents of those on the honor roll and those doing unsatisfactory work. In 1936 while the state was engaged in a curriculum study he advised the administrative cabinet, "We should do some independent surveying of the life of our Mennonite people with a view of curriculum adjustment to meet more directly our needs."

After the first year of the new administration, college work was again given—one year of it in 1933-34, and two years thereafter. By agreement with the state, students could get their credits validated by taking an additional nine hours of residence work in a state school.[27] In 1937-38 the deans of Hesston and Goshen Colleges collaborated to reorganize the curricula of the first two college years into a coordinated pattern of survey courses.

Of the faculty who began with the new administration, the president, Paul Erb, Mrs. Erb, and D. D. Driver served throughout the strenuous uphill years. J. N. Byler served five years, Maurice A. Yoder four, and J. Harold Smith four. Others listed in the faculty tenure chart served a lesser number of years.

In 1933-34 a college-level Christian workers' course was begun, tuition-free. In 1935 the executive committee of the Mennonite Board of Education recommended that

> Hesston College continue giving one year of college and may offer the second year if there is sufficient student demand, and sufficient faculty personnel to offer such work creditably and that any larger offerings involve no change in the school's financial program.[28]

In the same year the Board also recommended

> that it be the first aim of each institution under the Board to maintain an attitude of loyalty to God and the standards of the Church; and, as far as consistent with this policy, to conform in all possible ways with the requirements for standardization by recognized accrediting agencies.[29]

Student activities during these years were typical. In 1933-34 students began advocating a student council; the bookkeeping class under J. N. Weaver organized and for two years administered a Students' Commercial Bank; the Y, whose annual drive offerings rose from $100 to $500 during the six years, sent Gospel teams into the new mission stations in the Ozarks, two student colporteurs into the Arkansas-Tennessee hills, and teachers and support to a Sunday School at Medora, Kansas, and to the new Hutchinson, Kansas mission. The Y made persistent efforts to establish a continuous teaching program in the colored and the Spanish section of Newton.

In 1934-35 the literary societies were revived, the Excelsior and Philomathean in the academy and the Bryan-Delphian in the college. Although occasionally there were informative content programs, many consisted chiefly of entertaining experience accounts. During 1937-38 a Poetry Club existed and a peace oratorical contest occurred. A broom factory was organized on the campus to give work to students. For several years it supplied brooms to the townsfolk. In 1933-34 citizen-

117

Willie Helmuth and Fred Grove in the college dairy, about 1932.

ship awards were first given, but the granting of athletic awards was again postponed. The faculty favored the ordering of glass slides for use in clubs, classes, and pre-Easter services.[30] Out-of-state chorus tours were revived. On May 21, 1935, school colors were adopted—royal purple and lavender.[31]

In 1934 the twenty-fifth anniversary *Lark* was dedicated to A. L. Hess. The following anniversary program was given at the first all-school luncheon.

> Music: Quartet—Alvin Yordy
>   Paul Erb
>   Jesse Hartzler
>   M. D. Landis
> Part Played by Kansas-Nebraska Conference and the Mennonite Board of Education—L. O. King
> Locating the Site—T. J. Cooprider
> The Contribution of Hesston College and Bible School to the Program of the Church—J. N. Byler
> The Contribution of Hesston College and Bible School to the City—S. N. Nunemaker

Music: Quartet
Reminiscences—Grace Diller
          Lela Stutzman
          Vernon Shellenberger
          Gideon G. Yoder
Hesston College Twenty-five Years Hence—President Milo
                                Kauffman[32]

In 1935-36 an incident occurred that was sensational at the time. For an entire week the heating plant in the Administration Building was not in working order. The building was closed and classes were held in the dormitory and in faculty homes.[33]

The trend of the program and the spirit of the school are summarized thus by J. Harold Smith, a new teacher:

To analyze the school spirit is quite difficult. In the relationship of students and faculty a spirit of good fellowship combines with friendly interest. While there is respect for rank, there is no spirit of aloofness. The snobbish person is taboo.

Perhaps the most outstanding single characteristic of the entire school system is the emphasis placed on the development of a well-rounded personality, or more briefly, balance. Much

College milkmaids ready for a contest. Left to right: Verle Hershberger, Carrie Swartzendruber '31, Emma Chupp, Fannie Schrock '32 '40.

stress is placed on the growth of Christian experience and ample provision is made for it. Intellectual, social, and physical pursuits alike receive their due emphasis. Constant efforts are made to provide opportunity for the proper development of each one of these phases of our experience. The aim is to produce a character with strength sufficient to cope successfully with the difficulties of life.[34]

A student editorial describes the college spirit of the difficult years thus:

The recent depression wounded the countenance of good Hesston College. The onlookers passed her by. "There is Hesston College and Bible School," they said, "mortally wounded. . . ! We thought, before the depression crippled Hesston, that she would grow old and bless humanity but that is past . . . the old school is dying." They turned their eyes and forgot.

Yes, her countenance was wounded. You can still see the scars. But, Hesston was more than a countenance; she had a spirit. That spirit of Hesston College, unnoticed by onlookers, was never extinguished. Beneath her scarred countenance, her weathered buildings, her poverty-stricken campus . . . that spirit of staunch perseverance kept Hesston College alive. It was in the zeal of the faculty, in the prayers of some who were more than onlookers, and in the enthusiastic loyalty of undergraduates and alumni, that the never-say-die spirit had its abode.

Today, the onlookers say, "Look—the scar is nearly healed. Can it be that Hesston will recover?" Yes, passerby, Hesston College will recover. Just as there were men yesterday who looked beneath her countenance, so there are men today who will take up that spirit of progress and will make of Hesston College a wider and richer avenue of blessing to humanity. State accreditment is our next milepost. It is looming up encouragingly near.[35]

NORMALCY, 1938-1945

By 1938 the institution was emerging from its depression slump. In the seven succeeding years it continued its tasks on even ground. The college operated on income and annually applied $500 or more of its meager net profits to the debt carried into the Kauffman administration.[36] No major buildings were added, but its economic status was far above the 1932 level. Faculty members in 1938 were paid $90 per month; for the first time the president was voted one additional month's allowance for the summer, and teachers were given bonuses for advanced study;[37] the Bird Sanctuary was developed; campus trees were trimmed by specialists; a new cobblestone walk—which students who trod its bumpy, irregular surface for over a decade will surely remember— was laid

Green Gables and the cobblestone walk in the snow.

between Green Gables and the Administration Building; other sidewalks were laid; an electric refrigerator was donated to the Home Economics Cottage; and plans were being put into action for advertising, solicitation, and expansion.[38]

In 1941 a new forward move became evident. During the school term the business manager, L. L. Swartzentruber, and the president spent a great deal of time soliciting funds. S. N.

121

Nunemaker, the postmaster and an alumnus of the college, spoke to a community gathering on "The Value of Hesston College to the Community." The *Journal* of the year was alive with articles about "The Greatest Need of Hesston College," "Carrying Out a Building Program," and glowing tributes from loyal alumni of which the following are typical:

> To me, Hesston College is like a long-sought oasis. How refreshing the draught of sweet Christian fellowship with God's children is! How restful to be protected from the scorching sands by God-fearing instructors! My short stay here has revived my spirits and I am ready to face again the hardships of the desert journey ahead.[39]

> It's a terrific thrill to write for the one and only *Hesston College Journal* again. Nothing will ever find in my heart so cherished a spot as Hesston College. There is something about that inimitable Hesston spirit that gets to the very bottom of things and never lets go. My prayer is that this year's student body may enjoy the same glorious times we used to have and that they may keep the torch of brotherhood burning brightly.[40]

Industrial Arts Shop.

Reports of the year evidence growth, advertising, and exertion. The Industrial Arts Shop was erected during the summer, the Cooprider House was purchased and remodeled for a boys' dormitory, and a tile milkhouse and new well were added to the college dairy. A faculty round-table outlined "A Building Program for Hesston College." The administration and the town officials planned a policy of cooperation,[41] and as reported elsewhere the local board approved the A. L. Hess Trust proposal to transfer the title of the college farm to the Mennonite Board of Education.[42]

On November 28, 1941, the new Industrial Arts Shop was dedicated with the following program:

Place of Industrial Arts in Education .... Eli Stoltzfus
Place of Industrial Arts at Hesston College ...... Ivan R. Lind
Dedicatory Remarks .... President Kauffman[43]

In 1941-42 for the first time in the history of the school, boys and girls lived in separate buildings; only girls lived in

The Elms, a temporary dormitory for college men.

123

Green Gables. The boys had moved into the Cooprider House, now named "The Elms," and into neighboring homes. On first floor the north wing of Green Gables was converted into a commercial room.

Minor campus improvements and economic stabilization continued. Because the gymnasium had been wrecked by a tornado in the summer of 1942, a new one was built, largely from insurance payments. Green Gables was re-roofed. The president and business manager were active on the debt liquidation program. Notes in issues of the 1942 *Gospel Herald* awakened the constituency anew to the indebtedness of the college.

> Hesston College began to accumulate debt in 1913 to the amount of $532.92. This increased gradually until 1925, when it reached $12,450. This amount was then reduced to $3,900, when the Board of Education took it over in 1927. By September 1, 1935, when the Board again carried the accounts of the two schools (Hesston and Goshen) separately, the operating deficits of the depression years had raised Hesston's debts to $33,110. Since 1935, Hesston's debt has decreased to $29,661.[44]

> From 1924 to 1932 the Board borrowed $33,000 for Hesston's debt. Since 1932 both schools have operated on a balanced budget. Hesston built an Industrial Arts Shop and dedicated it free of debt. From 1932-1942 the schools have reduced their indebtedness. In June 1942, the Board started a Debt Liquidation Program with a $75,000 goal.[45]

In the same year, 1942, Church School Day, which has since become an annual occasion, was first observed. The new Debt Liquidation Program was proving effective. By October 24, $40,388.07 cash and pledges had been collected for the indebtedness of the college.[46] In 1943 a friend added $1,110 to be invested in bonds and held in trust for purchase of land for the school.[47] The college buildings that year were insulated and storm windows were placed on the north side of the Administration Building and Green Gables.[48]

124

The first *Journal* of the school year, 1944-45, contained this note: "The Board of Education has authorized Hesston College to study plans and dormitories, to secure an architect to draw up plans, and to present plans to the Executive Committee in December." Two solicitors, Edward Diener and G. G. Yoder, were on the field. The December *Journal* continued:

> The architects are now busy with plans for the new dormitory. Funds are being solicited for it . . . the new Bungalow is ready, a temporary home for college girls . . . not the new dormitory for which funds are being solicited. The new dormitory is to replace Green Gables as a home for the girls in the fall of 1946. Green Gables will then be the home of our young men.

The Bungalow, a temporary dormitory for college ladies.

As far back as 1919 there had been glowing preparations for a new dormitory for girls. Funds had been collected; a foun-

125

dation had been laid and had waited long years for the super-structure. In 1933 the foundation was uprooted and hauled away. The long dream for a new dormitory for girls seemed gradually to have faded away. Green Gables is still the home of the girls. The same issue of the *Journal,* December, 1944, explained carefully that the Bungalow was financed by personal donations and by college income, not by funds collected for the new dormitory.

Enrollment during these seven years, 1938-1945, did not increase rapidly. There were 43 junior college students in 1938-39; by 1941-42 there were 86; but through the war years the number decreased again to 41. Academy enrollment increased from 118 in 1938-39 to 197 in 1944-45. Special Bible Term enrollment had reached its peak in 1938-39 and declined gradually during the next six years, largely because the college was already overcrowded. Although there had been 20 junior college graduates in 1938-39, by 1943-44 and 1944-45 there were only 4 and 5. The number of academy graduates rose from 26 in 1938-39 to 68 in 1943-44.

During these years the curriculum was constantly being modified and expanded. The junior college was again accredited. The education curriculum for securing teaching certificates was outlined by the state. General survey courses had been planned in cooperation with Goshen College. By 1941-42, the catalog contained suggestive terminal curricula—teacher training, home economics, general business administration, and secretarial work. In 1943, Hesston College was authorized by the Board to grant A.A. degrees to junior college graduates.[49] In 1945 the 6-4-4 plan was adopted—a reorganization by which the junior college included four years, the first two years of college and the two upper grades in high school. Grades nine and ten were called the preparatory school.

126

A few developments occurred in the Bible curriculum, largely as a result of the establishment of a seminary at Goshen. In 1942 the following note appeared in the minutes of the Board of Education:

> By joint action of Goshen College and Hesston College, authorized and approved by the Mennonite Board of Education, a five-year program of preparation for Christian work and service in the Mennonite Church has been set up, in which Hesston students will transfer to Goshen for the last two years. . . . This informal cooperation of the past eight years has been transformed into a formal agreement by which the program of preparation for church service in the two schools is integrated.[50]

By 1941-42 four hours of Bible were required for graduation from junior college, one unit for high school graduation, and a one-hour Bible subject was compulsory each semester.[51]

To both the college and academy curricula new and varied subjects were added. A first aid course for the community, taught by the local physician began in 1938-39; in 1940-41 new courses in family living, Spanish, office practice, accounting, college life, woodworking, elementary school arts, Christian education, and homiletics were added.[52] The next year there were more additions—speed-writing, agriculture, mechanical drawing, introduction to education, arithmetic, Greek.

An enriched and varied curriculum demanded more teachers. A number were already of long tenure. Coming in from the previous administration were Paul Erb and Alta Mae Erb, D. D. Driver, Mary Miller, J. N. Byler, Maurice A. Yoder, Verna Enns Guengerich, and Elizabeth Gish Yoder. J. Harold Smith had come in 1934-35, Samuel Swartz in 1935, Bertha Nitzsche in 1936-37, Ivan R. Lind in 1938-39, J. H. Koppenhaver and John P. Duerksen in 1939-40, Wilmer Landis and Eli Stoltzfus in 1941-42, Ethel Climenhaga in 1943-44, and in 1944-45

127

Edwin I. Weaver, Eva Yeackley, Melva Kauffman, Verna Burkholder, Lois Litwiller and Marian Messner.

By 1938-39 a call came from Goshen College for Paul and Alta Mae Erb, who had practically grown up with the institution and become foundation parts of it. At the end of the first semester in 1940-41, Paul Erb, the dean of the college, transferred to Goshen College. He had enrolled as a student in Hesston College in 1910, the second year of the existence of the school. By 1913-14 he was listed as an assistant teacher, and in 1924 after Noah Oyer, the second dean of the college, went to Goshen, Paul Erb at the age of 30 was appointed acting dean. For four years during the absence of Dean Edward Yoder he served as acting dean and for eight more years after Edward Yoder went to Goshen he was dean of the institution. During these years he did practically full-time teaching. During the difficult years his continuous progressive adjustments of the curriculum, his straightforward resourceful facing of problems, his tireless efforts to advance along all fronts, and his buoyant faith and optimism were major factors in holding the institution together. Many alumni remember him as an inspiring, creative teacher. He organized the first extended chorus tours. Gaul's oratorio, "The Holy City," was first sung twice in 1914 and again in 1917. From 1923 to 1956 it was sung annually at commencement by the all-school chorus and home-coming alumni and for many years Paul Erb was the director. To his ex-students he is still an integral part of the institution. A student wrote, "Now he is leaving us; but we shall still have the culture, the religious philosophy, the spirit of charity he has shown us."[53]

To Alta Mae Erb the institution owes no lesser debt. She joined the faculty as early as 1912-13 and remained with it for 31 years. In the early years she taught a variety of subjects,

Alta Mae Erb, instructor, 1912-1918; 1919-1943; and Paul Erb, instructor, 1913-1941; acting dean, 1924-1928; and fourth dean, 1932-1941.

served as librarian for fifteen years, sponsored a strong creative forensics program, and served as preceptress of the girls' dormitory until her marriage in 1917. Normal training in high school was her particular interest, and when the institution

129

became a college in 1918 she was the head of the education department and held the position until 1942. Her courses were thorough, rich, and varied. She planned, organized, worked to capacity, and inspired her students to work. To her students she became the authority; they knew that she knew. She planned public programs through which varieties of student talents were discovered and developed. She sponsored annual art exhibits and through various activities during the display fostered art appreciation. She organized work parties during wartime Christmases at which all students were kept busy, enjoyed themselves, and made and packaged in one evening an unbelievable supply of relief materials to be sent to stricken peoples. The monthly faculty round-table discussions dealing with the improvement of classroom instruction were the results of her influence. From her present position in Scottdale, Pennsylvania, she is still directing learning activities.

Ivan R. Lind, fifth dean, 1941-1949.

After Paul Erb left in mid-year, 1940-41, to teach English at Goshen College, Ivan R. Lind became dean and remained in the office until his resignation for further study in 1949. During his deanship the curriculum became increasingly practical; terminal courses and the 6-4-4 plan of junior college organization were instituted.

There were other administrative and organizational developments during these years. In 1938-39 Amos Gingerich, the business manager, resigned; and L. L. Swartzentruber was appointed to succeed him. The next year the local board was organized to include ten members—H. A. Diener, President Milo Kauffman, Charles Diener, Earl Buckwalter, C. A. Vogt, O. O. Miller, A. N. Troyer, L. L. Swartzentruber, D. A. Yoder and Paul Erb.[54] In 1939-40 a student personnel department was organized and administered by J. H. Koppenhaver. The same year a two-day orientation program and a student health service were instituted. The next year a teacher retirement plan was outlined; and a dormitory council, organized under a student-government plan, began activities.[55] J. P. Duerksen took over the direction of the choruses after Paul Erb left, and in 1941-42 began a radio broadcast "The Hesston College Hour," sponsored by local business firms and school organizations. In 1943-44 Cooprider Hall was rechristened "The Elms," a name handed in by J. Harold Smith during a campus contest. In 1942-43 the first religious counselor was appointed, Ladies' Tea and Men's Mixer became a part of the orientation program, and a campus snack shop was set up and supervised by the personnel department.

In 1942-43 L. L. Swartzentruber, the business manager, resigned; and for two years thereafter the president served as business manager. During a part of the year, 1945-46, Paul Wittrig was business manager. In 1946 Daniel E. Kauffman, the grandson of Daniel Kauffman and T. M. Erb, who both had much to do with the birth of the college, was appointed as business manager and has served the school in that office since then. In 1944-45 a statement of school philosophy and objectives was formulated. The same year J. P. Duerksen, the music director, was called to C.P.S. Camp, and for the first time in the history of the school the choruses had a woman director, Verna Burkholder. Free mimeographing services were first furnished to the teachers in 1944-45.

The classes during these years had a number of memorable projects. The constitution classes held congress sessions and later visited the state legislature. The English III class consisting of sixty students in 1943-44 held a trial of Oliver Goldsmith in an English coffee house with Samuel Johnson in charge; and at Christmas the same class gave the Scrooge play, which has been given every year since then. The college speech class practiced storytelling to invited child-audiences. Chorus tours were made into the northern United States and on into Canada. The juniors for the first time tried to earn their junior-senior banquet money. Special Bible Term students started *The Spotlight,* their annual, in 1939-40. College freshmen and sophomores held annual debates. Literary societies during the art exhibit put on weekly art appreciation programs. Other student activities gave evidence of vitality. The Y had mission projects in Wichita, Hutchinson, and Medora. The Christian Workers' group spent a week or more in the Kansas City Mission and Children's Home. A group led by Richard Showalter, Y president in 1940-41, attempted to establish permanent work in a Negro district. The daily dormitory prayer meetings were still held during these years,[56] and the Thursday evening all-school devotionals were still being a source of spiritual strength to students. One *Journal* reporter referred to them as "The Thursday evening devotions, perhaps one of the most interesting and inspirational meetings on our campus."[57] Literary societies were still in operation; but clubs were springing up through student and faculty cooperation—in 1940-41 a Home Economics Club and Kwick Kamera Klique; in 1942-43 an Expression Club; in 1943-44 an Art Club; and in 1944-45 a Speech Club. Gradually clubs were replacing the long-lived literary societies.

A number of episodes of more or less significance occurred during these years. In 1939-40, A. C. Gingerich of the Maple-crest Turkey Farms first donated turkeys for the college Christmas dinner and has done it annually since then. To the Christmas dinner that year all students brought gifts for the new Spanish mission in La Junta, Colorado. Jenny, one of "the team of little mules" purchased by A. L. Hess and donated to the college in its first years was described in a "Did You Know" column in a 1942 *Journal* as "Jenny, the college mas-

Jenny and the college milk delivery cart.

cot and the milk boy's able assistant, is supposed to be the oldest mule in captivity."[58]

In 1940 it was necessary for Maurice A. Yoder to have his second leg amputated. In 1941-42 the administration first "decided to fly the flag every day if weather permits;"[59] and Dean Lind organized a war emergency program to abbreviate the school term. There were Saturday classes and a short Easter vacation and school closed on May 12 instead of June 2. The same year a tornado struck Hesston, destroyed three barns near the town, ruined crops, tore to pieces the college gymnasium and banged parts of it into the Industrial Arts Shop and the Home Economics Cottage. The roof of Green Gables was badly damaged, 100-200 campus windows broken, many trees blown down, and the college wheat and oats crops totally destroyed.[60]

In 1943-44 a strong student vote changed the school colors to white and maroon.[61] On October 18 of the same year the *Gospel Herald* office received a telegram from President Kauffman: "The greatest revival in the history of Hesston College has swept our campus touching the lives of every student and faculty member as a result of prayer throughout the church. We call for united prayers that this revival may spread throughout the country."[62] During the revival a "sin-burning" bonfire was held in the Bird Sanctuary; and printed slogans, "Remember October 18" were hung above all classroom doors. A college newsletter in the spring stated, "During the remainder of the year a special effort for evangelism is being put forth. . . . Each Sunday evening we enjoy the privilege of a revival service."[63] In 1944-45 class educational tours began. All classes for one or two school days visited city industries and culture centers. The tours were continued until 1958-59, when they were replaced by course field trips. On January 30, 1944, funeral services for D. H. Bender, the first president of Hesston College, were held in the college chapel with Milo Kauffman, Paul Erb, and J. G. Hartzler in charge.

Slowly, steadily during these years the college had collected forces and awaited direction. Again the cloud had taken form and was moving forward. The institution was ready, eager for the advance.

THE BOOM YEARS, 1945-1951

In the postwar years there was ready money. People's hearts had been opened by relief-giving, and the needs of those in war-torn countries were gradually becoming less acute. The pillar of cloud indicated a time ripe for the execution of a building program, and the administration was quick to follow its leading. The 1945 summer issue of the *Journal* carried a large picture of the architect's plan of a new dormitory for girls. The president spent a strenuous summer attending board meetings and conferences and soliciting funds. By the end of 1945, $60,000 in cash and pledges had been gathered; and the Board of Education gave the "Go ahead orders" for a new dormitory. The building was to begin in the early spring under the direction of F. G. Roupp, who had been in charge of all the major campus constructions after the first one.[64]

In February the Board of Education met, approved plans for the building of a new auditorium-gymnasium, and authorized the college to use in the construction, recently purchased material from government buildings.[65] The new building plan was in no way to detract from the dormitory plan; all donations during the year were to be used for the girls' dormitory.[66] But as a result of World War II, construction materials for a dormitory were not available. The next issue of the *Journal* was replete with plans for the new auditorium-gymnasium.

The community was interested; it was to be located east of the farm home; and the dining room and kitchen were to be in its basement.[67] A month later the community was given a fellowship dinner by the college in appreciation of its "liberal response" to the appeal for auditorium-gymnasium funds.[68]

In February a building committee was appointed "to study the placement of other buildings."[69] The new committee suggested a further complication—"wings to the Administration Building."[70]

The September *Journal* of the next school year, 1946-47, reported, "Building program for the Hesston Auditorium-Gymnasium is encouraging ... materials arriving ... workmen laboring." The November *Journal* continued, "Full speed ahead in Auditorium-Gymnasium. All materials here ... Frank Roupp contractor." The January 20, 1947 *Journal* carried on the same note, "Contributions received for Auditorium-Gymnasium ... One alumnus $1,000, one $300 ... Many $100."

The January 27, 1947 minutes of the college administrative committee record:

> It was suggested we need to be thinking in terms of a complete building program by 1950 . . . the auditorium should be finished during the summer of 1947. The dormitory should be completed in 1948. This would be possible by borrowing money from the Mennonite Finance Corporation on a twenty to thirty year basis.

In February, 1947, the expiration of the girls' dormitory dream began. The February 3 *Journal* carried a half-hearted reference to the dormitory:

> Hesston is now erecting an auditorium-gymnasium ... planning to begin work on a girls' dormitory when materials and labor are more plentiful . . . also studying need for more library space and classrooms.

The March 1, 1947 *Journal* reported:

> The Board of Education meets on the campus for the first time . . . February 17-18. . . . After completion of A. L.

Hess Memorial Hall, the new auditorium-gymnasium, plans should be made for building a new girls' dormitory for 100 to 125 ladies and a Health Center. . . . Another immediate need is classrooms, library, chapel, and offices.

In the March 15 issue the *Journal* continued, "The framework of the auditorium-gymnasium is nearing completion. Sheet rock ceiling is being put on . . . acoustical tile later on. . . ."

Funds for auditorium chairs were solicited from alumni in repeated letters advocating the slogan, "Every alumnus a chair," and reporting the number subscribed and the number yet needed. One alumnus remarked in a class letter, "I'd surely like to come to commencement at Hesston and see all those

Poster for the "Every Alumnus a Chair" campaign.

chairs." The Hesston Homemaker's Club furnished kitchen equipment. The new dining room was furnished with tables having linen formica tops trimmed in stainless steel. The local boys, "Hayseeds," donated an electric scoreboard for the gymnasium. The Board of Education had authorized the president to borrow $5,000 from the endowment fund of Hesston College to pay for four "garden houses"—prefabricated houses to be used for faculty homes—to sell lots from college property, and to move the old gymnasium and convert it into a college boys' dormitory.[71]

The pillar of cloud had moved so fast in the two years after the long hard years of tarrying that it had been difficult to

Hess Memorial Hall.

follow. There were many turns it could have taken. Why the pillar again moved away from the construction of a girls' dormitory as it had in the first administration is a matter we leave to Him who moves the pillar along its route.

Hess Memorial Hall was dedicated on November 7, 1947, with the following program:

Chairman	President Kauffman
Congregational Singing	Led by J. P. Duerksen
Devotions	A. G. Horner
What This Building Means	
To the Student	Evan Oswald
To the Community	M. M. Vogt
To the South Central Conference	H. A. Diener
To the Alumni	Wilbert Nafziger
Greetings from Goshen College	President E. E. Miller
Music	A Cappella Chorus
Dedicatory Address	D. A. Yoder, President
	Board of Education
Dedicatory Prayer	Nelson E. Kauffman
Thank Offering	
Benediction	
Open House and Refreshments[72]	

The plaque on the rear wall of the auditorium-gymnasium bears this inscription:

This building honors the memory of A. L. Hess, 1861-1920, pioneer citizen and public-spirited community builder for whom the city of Hesston was named; kindly neighbor and genial friend of the young; patron of Christian education, whose philanthropy helped determine the site of this school, and whose continuing generosity and counsel were a source of strength to its early leaders.

The new building was finished, dedicated, paid for at a total cost of $108,051.22, and the school was operating without deficit.[73] And almost immediately new building needs projected themselves. The 1947-48 catalog stated that the old gymnasium had been converted into a rooming house, Ath. Hall; and that funds were being raised for "the proposed new girls' dormitory;" work on the building, it was hoped, would begin by spring 1948. The September *Journal* of 1948 took up the dormitory refrain, "The Board of Education has given approval of the construction of a new dormitory. Solicitation will start in the fall." Even before the note above was printed, this little item had appeared in the November 25, 1947 *Gospel Herald* in the "Mennonite Board of Education Items:" "Hesston College is in need of a new administration building with classrooms and library space . . . and a new dormitory." During the year a committee of consultants invited to the college to study the organization had suggested, among other needs, an inexpensive science building.[74]

The catalog of 1948-49 had mentioned "the proposed new girls' dormitory . . . considerable funds have been raised . . . ." But by December 11, 1948, the Mennonite Board of Education had authorized the erection of the new science hall. Construction was to begin as soon as $25,000 had been collected.[75]

By the spring the business manager released plans for seven campus improvements: "the moving of Ath. Hall, a new science hall, a new health unit, a new athletic field, two new faculty homes, curtains for the auditorium stage, and furniture for the student lounge."[76]

Before the 1948-49 school year closed $48,000 had been collected for the science hall—$18,000 in cash and $30,000 in pledges. The building committee was appointed—President Milo Kauffman, Daniel E. Kauffman, H. A. Diener, Allen White, Lyle E. Yost, and Dr. Fred Brenneman. The architect was employed, Frank Roupp was again contractor, and at commencement time the president "threw the first shovel of dirt at a ground-breaking for the new science building."[77]

In the fall of 1948 science hall progress reports began appearing regularly in the *Journal*:

Construction began on the Science Building November 8. Frank Roupp, contractor, drove the first corner stake laying out the extremities of the building . . . brick and cinder blocks outside . . . interior walls cinder block . . . no plastering . . . asphalt tile floor . . . good insulation . . . acoustical treatment.[78]

By December 3, the *Journal* reported, "50,000 bricks have been laid for the new Science Hall. It is being built on the pay as you go plan." By June, 1949, the science hall was entirely enclosed; then building was discontinued because of a lack of funds.[79] Construction was not resumed until January, 1951. In the spring, students worked two school days for science building funds and brought in a total of $7,638.93, "enough to continue work on the science building. $15,000 more is needed to equip it."[80]

A church building, too, had long been a dream. The movement toward reality began in 1947, when the college congregation at its annual business meeting had passed a motion to build a new church. As a result of ensuing discussions a co-ordinating committee consisting of representatives from the local congregation, the college, and the Board of Education was chosen in 1948. A plan had emerged for a church-chapel building to serve the needs of the local congregation and to provide a chapel for the college and rooms for its Bible department.[81] Frank Roupp was employed with his son, Paul Roupp, to supervise construction, which was to begin as soon as $50,000 had been collected. The college assumed $80,000 of the cost. Annual church contributions of $30,000 were to be established as "basic and normal."

Heartening spurs to the campus improvement drive of these years were special donations. The agriculture class of 1945-46 planted blue grass, shrubs, forsythia on the grounds. The class of 1945-46 gave an addressograph to the school and a filing cabinet for the president's office. Jonas Kidder of North

The Bird Sanctuary.

Dakota gave a $1,000 annuity, J. A. Schowalter forty acres of land adjoining the Hesston College farm as "an endowment investment," Dr. Paton Yoder a twelve volume set of *A History of American Life* by Schlesinger and Fox, Mrs. Lena Rodgers and the graduating classes of 1949 the curtains for the auditorium stage, Edward Kanagy and Lewis Martin the acoustical tiling between the dining room and the auditorium in Hess Hall, the faculty the furniture and folding doors for the student lounge, Lyle E. Yost and other interested alumni a Steinway grand piano, the Hesston Homemakers a remodeling and refurnishing of the dean of women's living quarters, and Carl Magnuson bonus checks for each teacher.

The enrollment during these years of campus development did not increase markedly. More college students came—40, 83, 100, 109, 85, 97—consecutively during the years, 1945-1951; fewer academy students came—199, 208, 155, 154, 165, 150. Special Bible Term enrollments were also irregular. In

1945-46, because of a lack of dormitory room, there were only 18. In the five years following, there were 47, 78, 59, 44, 56. The number of junior college graduates increased after the war years. In 1946, five girls but no boys were graduated; in the years following, graduates numbered 12, 29, 29, 28, 27. The number of high school graduates decreased slightly after the war years—62, 67, 64, 50, 65, 35.

Personnel changes in the administrative staff occurred during these six years. Ivan R. Lind, who had served as dean for eight years, resigned in 1949 and was succeeded by Walter E. Oswald. Paul Wittrig, the business manager in 1945-46, resigned because of ill health and was succeeded in the fall of 1946 by Daniel E. Kauffman. John H. Koppenhaver, the first personnel director of the college, resigned in 1947 after seven years of service to take up missionary work in Argentina; he was replaced by Walter E. Oswald.

Faculty and staff additions and changes were numerous. In 1945 for the first time the institution had a trained librarian, Esther Weber, with a B.S. in library science. Previous to her coming to Hesston College, she had served as a cataloger in the Pennsylvania State College Library and as librarian at the New School for Social Research in New York City.[82] The same year Walter E. Oswald, M.A., University of Chicago, a teacher and administrator of wide experience, joined the faculty, and served the institution in various ways during his nine years' stay. Among others who came during these years were Glenn L. Hershberger, Alice Buckwalter, Trusie Zook, Orpha Zimmerly, Anna Shirey, Naomi Brubaker, Freedley Schrock, John Steiner, Paul E. Yoder, Cleda Holdeman, Christine Blosser, Gladys Winn who served as registrar 1948-52, Gideon G. Yoder, Milton Vogt, Laurence Horst, Vincent J. Krabill, Willard Conrad, Clayton Beyler, Ellen M. Miller, Leonard L. Lichti, Evelyn I.

Rouner, and Harold Yoder. Bertha Nitzsche, who had given the institution long years of service in various capacities, left the college in 1950 to serve as dietitian in the La Junta Hospital.

A number of administrative practices and policies developed during these six years. The first faculty fall conference was held in 1945.[83] Foreign students first began coming in 1946 through M.C.C. sponsorship.[84] A visual education policy was adopted;[85] a class sponsorship system organized.[86] In 1946-47 the college began paying Blue Cross fees for faculty members and their families. After an administrative attempt to fit class banquets and commencement programs into the 6-4-4 junior college plan, high school banquets and graduation programs were revived in 1946-47.[87] The same year a reorganized student council received faculty approval, and a faculty student-counseling system was put into operation.[88] Tuition fees for C.P.S. men were paid by the Mennonite Board of Missions and Charities for the length of time they had spent in camp, up to twenty-seven months.[89] In the same year began the first Annual Midwestern Youth Rally at Thanksgiving time,[90] the forerunner of the Annual Thanksgiving Homecoming, which in 1958-59 was again changed into a youth conference.

In the fall of 1944 the faculty adopted the proposed plans of the round-table committee for a program of study to formulate a statement of philosophy and objectives for the institution.[91] During the year one evening per month was given to this study. In the summer of 1945, while Melva Kauffman, the instructor in education, was studying for her master's degree at the University of Wisconsin, Dean Lind asked her to incorporate the discussions of the faculty and the principles of education into a written statement of philosophy and objectives. Miss Kauffman first introduced her paper to the faculty in the fall of 1945,[92] the same year the University of Kansas was reevaluating the junior college for accreditation.[93]   Throughout that year and the next the proposed statement was studied and revised.   A faculty meeting note of October 29, 1946, states, "the study of the proposed educational objectives was resumed and completed."   A motion "referred it to an editorial board." Nothing further was done with the statement until Walter E. Oswald, who became dean in 1949, discovered it, thought it good, and had it published in the college catalog.   The "Educational Philosophy and Objectives" as it was approved after the faculty study is included in the appendices.

In the 1947-48 school term a committee of educators and administrators was invited to the campus "to study the program now in operation and to give suggestions for a forward-going program."   The committee consisted of Jesse P. Bogue of Washington, D. C., executive secretary of the American Association of Junior Colleges and editor of the *Junior College Journal;* W. A. Black, head of the department of education and psychology at the State Teachers College, Pittsburg, Kansas; and Ernest E. Miller, president of Goshen College, Goshen, Indiana.   The committee recommended that the institution consider discontinuing the first two years of high school, narrowing the base of operations and stressing quality work within its framework, studying the effectiveness of the 6-4-4 plan, limiting teaching loads of administrative officers, and providing more adequate salaries and facilities.[94]

The Board in 1947-48 adopted a policy "regarding the consistent use of musical instruments." The school should give "private instruction offered on standards of academic accreditment . . . should get faculty instructors . . . organize techniques for developing and improving our church along traditional lines and strongly to promote the same."[95]   On December 19, 1949, after the school had received a gift of a new

Steinway piano, the faculty "favored its use for other than church purposes,"[96] and on May 3, 1950, "granted permission for its use in the rendition of *The Messiah* and *The Holy City*."[97]

Early in the 1947-48 term, the cabinet system of administration was abolished, department heads were elected by faculty groups,[98] and a consistent salary scale based on training was organized by Dean Oswald. It was not until 1947 that at the request of the local board a Constitutional Revision Committee voted to study the "best alternative to a Local Board." The committee reported to the Board of Education on February 18, 1947:

> . . . the committee has not come to a common mind . . . but does unanimously agree on strengthened powers and wider duties of the Executive Committee of the Board in relation to local administration of the schools.

After continued study the committee offered the following recommendation: "That the constitutional provision for the appointment and membership of the following standing committees be suspended. . . . local school committees . . . local board and Welfare Committees."[99] After the recommendation, the local board discontinued activities. A year later the Board adopted a new constitution in which a particular effort was made "to coordinate all areas of education promoted by the Mennonite Church . . . to make more collaboration possible."[100]

The faculty study committee in 1947-48 began an intensive study of the campus religious life, a self-study survey sponsored by the Religious Welfare Survey Committee of the Mennonite Board of Education.[101] In 1949-50 the institution before joining the American Association of Schools of Religious Education for the first time attempted to articulate its religious philosophy

146

and objectives.[102]   The statement adopted is included in the appendices.

Among other innovations of the period were the allowance of an annual $10 professional fee to each teacher, the employment of a staff taxidermist, an annual workdays program, and taking advantage of social security benefits for teachers.

Curriculum adjustments continued through these years.   In 1946-47, Nora Miller, who was then superintendent of the La Junta School of Nursing, presented a proposal for cooperation between the Mennonite colleges and the nursing school, especially for those sciences which the teachers of the nursing school were not qualified to teach.[103]   The next year one science course required for nurses, microbiology, was added to the curriculum.   By 1950 a pre-nursing program for the college had been effected cooperatively with the La Junta, Colorado Hospital and the Bethel Deaconess Hospital at Newton, Kansas, and the State Board of Examiners of Kansas, Missouri, and Colorado.   Mature girls who had missed high school could take G.E.D. tests and register in pre-nursing courses.[104]   By the plan which the La Junta Hospital had previously arranged with the Colorado State Board, students could take at Hesston College a pre-nursing course in the basic sciences and thereby reduce to thirty months actual residence at the hospital and in other affiliations.[105]

A continuous effort was being made to prove the 6-4-4 plan effective, as the Bogue Committee had suggested.   Grades nine and ten were the preparatory school; grades eleven, twelve, thirteen and fourteen were the junior college and were called the freshman, sophomore, junior, and senior years, respectively. Units of terminal curricula were set up in the annual catalogs— liberal arts, teacher training, home economics, general business

147

Men's Chorus, 1946-1947. John P. Duerksen, director.

administration, secretarial, nursing, agriculture. An effort was made to minimize high school graduation activities, and to make graduation from junior college with an A. A. degree traditional. In 1948-49 the Board of Education recommended the following program: four years of high school, grades 9-12; junior college liberal arts preparatory school, 13-14; four years Bible Course leading to a Th.B., 13-16; terminal agriculture course leading to a major, 11-14; elementary normal training course leading to a B.S., 13-16; a campus model and practice elementary school.[106]

The plan for a B.S. in education was dropped because of the objections offered by the Department of Public Instruction, and the establishing of a laboratory school was postponed to preserve wholesome public relations. In 1949-50 the Board of Education authorized the college to give a four-year Bible course leading to a degree of Bachelor of Religious Education, B.R.E. The same year two students were graduated from the course.

A coordinated Winter Bible School program to effect cooperation between schools was organized in 1945. All courses were arranged under four heads—Bible study, Bible doctrines, church history, and practical work—and were planned for a three-year cycle, for terms of both six and three weeks. One unit of credit represented completion of twelve lessons with forty-five minute class periods and one hour of study per period. By following the plan, schools could freely exchange credits.

With the addition of a trained physical education teacher in 1946, a school physician in 1944, and a standard health center in 1948, a more generally effective health program was put into operation. To encourage more students to exercise more frequently and to stimulate interest in types of recreation that would continue into adult life, a committee headed by John Steiner, the new athletic director in 1947, put into operation a variety of minor sports—ping pong, shuffleboard, horseshoe, archery, croquet, badminton, quoits, cross country, handball, baseball, free throw, swimming. With the help of interested alumni an enlarged athletic field was planned and prepared.

Other new course offerings were being added annually—modern languages, art, homemaking, speech, business, shop, commerce, voice and piano. Added evening classes were arranged for adults. A strong forensics program was directed by Paul E. Yoder. Monthly round-table discussions on the improvement of instruction continued throughout the years in faculty meetings.

Student activities were typical. Clubs continued replacing the old literary societies. Annual social talks by outside speakers, the Scrooge play at Christmas time, the Thanksgiving Youth Rally, relatively distant educational tours, the ducking of engaged fellows in the fishpond, the wearing of graduation gowns, extended chorus tours, participation in the state WCTU-sponsored anti-alcohol contest—all became a part of school traditions. The Y reached out farther in its activities. A mission church was established in Eureka Gardens, a Y outpost in Wichita, and mission activities were started in Orienta, a needy section near the mission church. The annual Y drives now resulted in offerings of $1500 to $1800. In 1946 the organization purchased a new Ford station wagon to facilitate its extension services. Its emergency relief committee occasionally gathered groups to help in the Newton M.C.C. Center, promoted a "hanky" drive to gather handkerchiefs for the four postwar Mennonite Children's Homes in France, arranged a Christmas clothing collection that was sent to a German school previously attended by a German classmate.

An art class sketching in the Bird Sanctuary under the instruction of Alice Buckwalter.

Other organizations too were public-spirited. The Art Club, during National Picture Week, under the sponsorship of Alice Buckwalter, daily posted reproductions of masterpieces with informative captions. As a project the group decorated the dining room walls with colorful murals depicting campus scenes. The Student Council sent five representatives to the National Students' Organization, planned all-school parties, dress-up suppers, clean-up and anti-noise campaigns; helped supply funds for phonograph records for the Student Lounge, added attractions to the Bird Sanctuary, put metal glides on the library chairs, successfully promoted more open library hours and the faculty's marching with graduating classes at commencement. The speech class to promote campus courtesy produced and gave a play, "The Hick of Hampton College," and to show the effectiveness of returning good for evil the class gave a peace play, "The Friendly Kingdom." In 1949 the rendition of *The Holy City* by the all-school chorus received national recognition. "A report of it was made to music educators at the National Convention in Detroit, Michigan, last April and was so enthusiastically received that Alvin Reimer, music director at Stafford, Kansas, has asked for information and photographs to be formulated into a booklet for national distribution among music teachers."[107]

A number of memorable incidents occurred during these years. By the end of the year, 1948-49, D. D. Driver had served the institution twenty-five years. The 1950 *Lark* was dedicated to "Professor D. D. Driver for his faithful service in

D. D. Driver '16, '23, instructor in chemistry.

the mathematics and science departments and for his loyal support of the Hesston College ideal...." Not only had Mr. Driver taught mathematics and science; he had almost continuously served the alumni association and the local congregation in official capacity. In 1950 alumni and friends pooled funds and presented him a new Ford in appreciation for his selfless service.

In 1945-46 because the school for several weeks was quarantined for scarlet fever, students could not attend the Don Cossack concert given at Bethel College. To relieve the frustration of fellow students the seniors sponsored a party featuring a mock Don Cossack Chorus performance. To the ill in the infirmary they sent rival newspapers—"The Scarlet Evening Messenger" and "Scarletina's Scrapbook." To relieve anxious parents, friends of the afflicted took dictation through windows for letters to be sent home.[108]

In the fall of 1946 a defective heating system caused a fire in the Bungalow, the college girls' rooming house. The fire was first noticed at 10:45 a.m. on Sunday during church services. The Hesston fire truck appeared on the scene immediately and had extinguished the flames before the Newton firemen arrived. The property of the girls had been removed and thrown on heaps on the campus. Later the collection was taken to the Home Economics Cottage, the reception room, and the Industrial Arts Shop, where the girls spent many hours sorting out their own shoes, dresses, notebooks. For several months the twenty-eight girls lived in community homes while repairs were made.

On April 25, 1949, occurred an incident deeply impressive in college life. Glenn L. Hershberger, a young mathematics teacher, was teaching his algebra class. While at the blackboard explaining a problem, he slumped to the floor and was dead of a heart attack before the doctor arrived on the scene. For several weeks before, he had been unable to teach, but felt better and had begun his regular tasks again. He left a wife and unborn child to whom his salary for the remainder

Glenn L. Hershberger, instructor in mathematics and physical science, 1945-1949.

of the year was paid. The family requested no flowers but asked that funds be contributed instead to the J. D. Charles Science Hall. One room in the building has been dedicated to Glenn L. Hershberger.

In the spring of 1950 President Milo Kauffman handed to the Executive Committee of the Board a letter of resignation: "to make it possible for me to do more evangelistic work, for which I feel a greater conviction at this time than I do for administrative work."[109]

When the Board met in October one of its resolutions read:

> That we express our appreciation for the untiring, sacrificial, and conscientious service of Milo Kauffman as President of Hesston College and Bible School, and that we accept his resignation as President of that institution to be effective September, 1951.[110]

The college *Journal* paid the outgoing President this tribute:

> Milo Kauffman became president of Hesston College in 1932. Hesston College was then at her lowest in finances and morale. There was talk of closing her doors. He guided her through perilous times and maintained the original function of the institution. He could be severely criticized and yet keep on the right road as closely as he could rightly interpret.
>
> When he came, the campus had three buildings: Green Gables, Administration Building, a gymnasium. During his term of service an extended list of new ones were added— the Art Shop, a new gymnasium later moved and remodeled into Ath. Hall, the College Bungalow, five Garden Houses, plus two other faculty homes, Hess Memorial Hall, and J. D. Charles Hall. The faculty grew from five to twenty-five, students from 65 to 300; debts were paid, new departments, Home Economics, Education, Pre-nursing, four-year Bible course were added. He served as business manager, solicitor, evangelist, teacher, pastor, and bishop of the college congregation and maintained an A rating for the academy department and junior college accreditment.[111]

The 1950 college annual was dedicated to him: "In deepest appreciation for the nineteen years of faithful guidance of the school and prayerful concern for each student, we dedicate *The Lark* to President Milo Kauffman." The president himself in "My Last Message as President" said:

> It is not easy to step out of a place where one has spent his best years, but I do so gladly. I am humbly grateful for any contribution that under God I may have been able to make to the cause. I leave the position, confident that my successor, with the same cooperation, will be able to do a better job than I have been able to do. I want to ask for him the whole-hearted support of students, faculty, and friends of Christian education. The work of Hesston College is worthy of your prayers and support. I want to assure all that I will be as vitally interested in the future of Hesston College as ever. My prayer and earnest support will ever be for Hesston College and Bible School.

I am not saying farewell, for I am not quitting. I am merely changing positions on the team. Whether after a year's leave I am at Hesston or elsewhere, I will feel myself definitely a part of Hesston College and Bible School. I will continue to rejoice in her successes and be pained by her failures. So in closing I give to the students, faculty, and friends of Hesston College not my farewell, but my benediction.[112]

VI. THE ROTH ADMINISTRATION, 1951-1959

*. . . the Lord will go before you; and the God of
Israel will be your rearward.*   —Isaiah 52:12

The resignation letter of Milo Kauffman had asked for re-
lease to "be effective by September, 1950, if possible . . . no
later than September, 1951."[1] The Board in October, 1950, accepted the following recommendation of its Executive Committee:

> That we recommend the election of Roy D. Roth of East
> Peoria, Illinois, as President of Hesston College and Bible
> School to succeed Milo Kauffman, who has resigned, and that
> the time of change in the administration be arranged by the
> Executive Committee by September, 1951, or as early as pos-
> sible thereafter.[2]

The president-elect, Roy D. Roth, had received B.A., Th.B.,
and B.D. degrees from Goshen College in 1942, 1944, and
1947, and a Th.M. from Princeton Theological Seminary in
1947. Since that time he had served as pastor in an East Peoria,
Illinois congregation and had been notably active in sponsoring youth and choral groups. He had also served as instructor
in the Winter Bible Term at Goshen College and as secretary
of the Mennonite Board of Education.

According to Kansas law a college administrator needed, as
a prerequisite to the presidency, two years of teaching under
contract. To meet state requirements Roy D. Roth taught two
years at Hesston College as president-elect; and during that
time he acquainted himself with its personnel, its constituency,
and its purposes and policies. Dean Walter E. Oswald served
during those two years as administrative head of the institution

Roy D. Roth, instructor and president-elect of Hesston College, 1951-1953; third president, 1953-1959.

and of an administrative committee including the president-elect; Daniel E. Kauffman, the business manager; Leonard L. Lichti, dean of personnel; and Merle L. Bender, director of public relations.[3]

The academic developments in the two years Dean Walter E. Oswald was head of the college evidence his strong spiritual and professional fervor and his deep concern for lifting the institution to a high educational plane. He had come to Hesston in 1945 with a B.A. from Goshen College, an M.A. from the University of Chicago, four years of experience as principal of the Brookfield, Ohio High School and sixteen years as dean of boys in the Hillman Junior High School in Youngstown, Ohio.[4] During his first two years at Hesston he was an instructor in social science, from 1947-1951 dean of student personnel, from 1949-1953 dean of instruction; and during the last two years of his deanship he also served as administrative head of the institution. In 1954 the Historical Committee of Mennonite General Conference requested that he be released to serve in the archives of the Mennonite Church at Goshen, Indiana.

Dean Oswald cooperated closely with the president-elect. The forward planning so evident during the last two years of his leadership was no doubt strongly abetted by the new president. Two movements were evident during his deanship, a persistent professional emphasis and a decentralization of power. One of his ardent ambitions for the institution was to get its high school department accepted into the North Central Association of Colleges and Secondary Schools. Step by step he went before to prepare the way, to lead, to inform. On September 19, 1951, the administrative committee recommended "that we drop the 6-4-4 plan and inaugurate the usual 8-4-2 academic program and that immediate steps be taken toward NCA accreditation in the high school department." On the same day the faculty adopted the recommendation,[5] and by October 24 the Board had given the go-ahead signal on the proposed change.[6]

To gain high school membership in the North Central Association, Dean Oswald worked closely with state officials. Faculty meeting notes report that "Ralph Stinson, chairman of the Kansas State Committee of the NCA, encouraged us to stand up for our stated objectives and philosophy."[7] ". . . Ralph

159

Stinson, state supervisor of secondary instruction, here all day."[8]

Steps toward meeting acceptance requirements followed in rapid succession. An extensive prerequisite self-evaluation by both faculty and students was set in motion,[9] other state officials came to counsel,[10] students and faculty were urged by Dean Oswald to give a cordial reception to the state investigation committee. On March 5, 1952, the committee came—sixteen representatives of the NCA from various schools, to check faculty and student evaluations, make their own observations, and formulate their report.[11] Two days later Mr. Stinson assured Dean Oswald that

> the committee of the NCA voted yesterday to recommend your school for admittance into the NCA. The committee was favorably impressed with the attitude and conduct of the student body and the cordial reception by the staff. This, I think, influenced the committee more than any other feature of your school.[12]

On April 3, 1952, the high school was admitted as a member of the NCA.[13] Less than a year later, Dean Oswald was appointed a member of an NCA committee " . . . to review member high schools and to consider new applicants."[14]

His concern for the standing of the institution is evident in excerpts from his annual reports:

> 108 diplomas and degrees granted—one of the largest classes in the history of the school,
>
> unqualified renewed acceptance of the high school division into the NCA of Colleges and Secondary Schools,
>
> continued accreditment of junior college by the state department and by the University of Kansas,
>
> the first year we could report to the State Department of Education that our library holdings are just a few short of 10,000 volumes.[15]

Other efforts to lift standards and to share responsibilities were forwarded by his influence—the implementation of an all-faculty counseling system; the resurrection of a student council; divisional faculty meetings and department planning and reorganization of course offerings;[16] the offering of more night courses; the reinstating of an examination period at the end of each semester; sponsor and custodian censorship of films

Walter E. Oswald, sixth dean, 1949-1953.

shown instead of administrative control; moral and financial encouragement to attend professional meetings; and the securing of the services of recognized specialists. "Donald M. Sterling of the Menninger Clinic in Topeka spoke twice on 'Christian Social Standards.' He also led discussion groups and was available for private counseling."[17]

To his respect for learning and his concern for the institution

161

and its students the following typical excerpts from his speeches and writings will testify:

> For if we want a government of the people, by the people, and for the people, it must be by an enlightened citizenry. The most fertile soil upon which all absolute monarchies have flourished the most profusely is the soil of ignorance of the masses of people.

> To have a deep respect for, and a deep desire to acquire truth revealed or secular, it seems to me, is the first real mark of a truly educated person. To acquire truth, whether in the scientific laboratory or in the classroom, from the revealed Word, or any other place, costs something.

> Great scholars are great because they are willing to pay the price of greatness in the form of hard labor, of systematically probing into apparent truths, oftentimes spending years of steady application before the truth sought for is revealed.

> Just passing in and out of college doors for a few years is no proof of having an education.[18]

In the first 1952-53 chapel address he again counseled students that real education costs dearly.

> Rivers and streams twist and turn as they do because they always take the course of least resistance; they always take the easiest way. No river plows through a mountain; it goes around it. No stream climbs over rocks unless it flows downhill and doesn't have to make any effort to go over the rocks. Did it ever occur to you that there are people . . . like a running stream? They, too, are crooked because too many times they take the line of least resistance. What seems at the moment to be the easiest way is the way they choose.[19]

In a letter to the *Journal* editor he re-articulated his concern that the institution might not lose its way in the maze of school trends.

> Hesston College must ever strive to raise its educational, as well as spiritual standards, if it hopes to remain true to the high ideals of its founders.

> We are an educational institution, sponsored by the Mennonite Church. Students coming to Hesston should come primarily to get a well-rounded Christian education with all it implies. To attend Hesston College for any other purpose is wrong; it defeats the purpose of the school . . . .

> Athletics or any other activity should have as its chief goal
> to help students be better students.[20]

At the end of the 1953-54 school year Walter E. Oswald left the college. A note in the faculty meeting minutes of May 27, 1953, reports "Whereas Dean Walter E. Oswald has served faithfully . . . giving himself unstintingly . . . we express appreciation."

On May 31, 1953, during the commencement season the new president was inaugurated in a ceremony attended by a record audience among whom were state officials—Ralph Stinson, supervisor of secondary education, and Adel Throckmorton, state superintendent of public instruction; the president and vice-president of the Mennonite Board of Education; and official representatives from various church colleges and local organizations. Harry A. Diener, vice-president of the Board, presided at the program; O. O. Miller, the financial agent of the Board, gave the address on "We Are Laborers Together With God;" and Nelson E. Kauffman, the president of the Board, was in charge of the inauguration.[21]

In accepting the office, the new president invoked on his administration blessings from on high and inspiration from the leadership of the past.

> Let us first of all lift up our eyes unto the Lord, from
> whence cometh our help. Let us remind ourselves that if . . .
> Christ were not on our side, our striving would indeed be
> losing. . . .
> Those who labored together with God at Hesston in the
> past and who have now entered into their great Sabbath rest
> have given to us of this generation the perpetual benefit of
> inspired encouragement to press onward in the Lord's work.[22]

Since Dean Oswald had during his two years of service as head of the school advised the administration that he wished to withdraw from official duties after 1953, the administration as early as October 6, 1952, recommended to the Executive Committee of the Mennonite Board of Education that Justus G. Holsinger be appointed acting dean of instruction and begin service in September, 1953. The training and experience of Justus G. Holsinger included a B.A. from Bridgewater College, an M.A. from the University of Virginia, eight years of public school administration and teaching in Virginia, seven years as director of a Puerto Rico service program, the writing of a book, *Serving Rural Puerto Rico,* and two years of teaching at Bluffton College. He came to Hesston College in 1952, served as registrar the first year, and became dean the second.[23] In 1956 he received a Specialist in Education degree from the University of Kansas. In 1959 he was appointed by the Kansas Council of Church-Related Colleges as one of its six members on the Professional Advisory Committee to the State of Kansas study of higher education authorized by Senate

Justus G. Holsinger, seventh dean, 1953-1959.

Resolution Number 25, for "a study, survey, report, and recommendations regarding the state educational system, beginning with kindergarten and extending through college or university."

While attending the University of Kansas, the dean in preparation for his thesis organized in 1953 a plan for a two-year faculty study of the curriculum of Hesston College, a study based on the educational philosophy of Hesston College as revised in 1950. To each of five organized faculty groups were assigned problems taken from the statement of philosophy. Is the curriculum adequate in its offerings, and flexible and adaptable to each learner's needs? Does it contribute to the "whole" development of the student? Does it offer opportunity to discover vocational fields, and preparation toward a definite life work? Is the organization of curricular activities cooperative and democratic? Do the course offerings provide opportunity for the development of right attitudes toward God, self, family, friends, community, church, and state?

As a result of the study the faculty revised its statement of educational objectives. Dr. Cloy S. Hobson from the University of Kansas visited the campus and explained to the faculty the concept of general education, a term not used before in curriculum revision at Hesston College.

The general education objectives of the institution as revised stated that Hesston College through its curriculum strives to develop in each student spiritual maturity in preparation for maximum use in the church; habits of reflective, creative, and independent thinking; a respect for others and the ability to work cooperatively with them; the skills of communication— to listen with understanding, read with comprehension, write with clarity, and speak with meaning; a Christian concept and practice of stewardship of time, money, and property—including the wise use of leisure time; an appreciation of the aesthe-

165

The Fountain.

tic, through an understanding of literature, music, and art; an appreciation of man's physical and biological environment, and its relationship to man and God; an understanding of the rights and obligations of Christian citizenship; emotional health and character growth through an understanding of human behavior; physical fitness and health; productive skills necessary in everyday life—including the mathematical and mechanical skills; an understanding of the obligations of home life and the role of parenthood.

Through research carried on as a second phase of the study, certain conclusions were established to help in future curriculum planning. A large majority of Hesston graduates are actively engaged in church work. Many high school and junior college graduates marry within five years after graduation and assume the responsibilities of parents. A majority of junior college alumni continue their educational studies. Hesston College high school graduates rate well above the average of the State of Kansas, and the college students compare favorably with other college students of the nation.

This study served as a basis for strengthening the college curriculum. The mathematics program was improved; a course in fine arts was added and both it and literature were required for college graduation; more emphasis was placed on emotional health and an understanding of human behavior, on Christian citizenship training, on an understanding of Christian stewardship through instruction in Bible classes and chapel programs, on preparation for the role of parenthood in both high school and college courses.[24]

One of the outstanding conclusions of the study was that a college curriculum is dynamic and developmental—constantly changing to meet the varying needs of the youth and the community it serves.

Administrative Council, 1953-1957, left to right: Justus G. Holsinger, dean of instruction; Daniel E. Kauffman, business manager; Roy D. Roth, president; Leonard L. Lichti, dean of student personnel; Merle L. Bender, director of public relations.

167

A number of general trends became evident in the new administration. A strong operative organization grew apparent. Additions were made to the faculty and staff. Standing faculty committees were asked to articulate their objectives and student representatives were added to the committees. Chapel programs were evaluated, a list of specific chapel objectives formulated, and the programs planned according to schedule and pre-published weekly in the daily "communicator" sheet sent to teachers. The Faculty Fall Conference grew into a three-day retreat at a campground for faculty and staff families. The Youth Rally during the Thanksgiving season became a Home-Coming "in honor of all parents and alumni" with luncheons, programs, one-day open house with school in session, varsity-alumni and regional basketball games. Plans were begun in 1952 for the fiftieth anniversary of the college in 1959, and the writing of the fifty-year history was assigned. A five-day orientation for new students, a parent-faculty "get-acquainted" program,[25] outdoor graduation exercises, and the service of 1-W men on the campus began in 1953-54.[26] Each week the president sent to the faculty a mimeographed memo informing them of administrative plans and activities; and in December, 1952, he began sending to the constituency a four-page monthly periodical, *This Month,* to report happenings, developments, and concerns at the college.

To put into operation an effective supervision and guidance program, the administration reorganized the student personnel program. The dean of personnel after the 1953-54 term had no disciplinary duties. The deans of men and women were directly responsible to the president and had a student affairs committee for support and counsel in difficult cases.[27] Full-time religious counselors were employed, student handbooks were rewritten in more positive terms, and admission requirements became more precise. There was in the new administration a strong effort to conserve traditions and practices of the (Old) Mennonite Church. The following note signed by all faculty members appeared on the front page of *This Month* in September, 1953:

> We, recognizing a divine call to serve on the Hesston College and Bible School faculty, dedicate all our energies to Christ and His Church to teach in harmony with, and nothing contrary to, the doctrines of the Word and the historic principles of the Mennonite Church, to be active in leading students to deeper experiences with Christ so that they may respond to His call to fellowship and service, and to do our best to maintain a fervent spiritual and evangelistic atmosphere on the campus.

Simultaneously with such conservative emphases a progressive current became evident. There were teacher exchanges with other church colleges, chapel program exchanges, extramural games with other church colleges, and speakers and teachers from other church groups. Dramatics, which had been limited to a Scrooge scene fitted into a Bible Christmas setting, was encouraged in clubs and classes; and attendance at plays in surrounding colleges was no longer questioned.[28] One, rather than two, annual series of revival meetings was scheduled, and a Spiritual Emphasis Week was observed, devoted largely to chapel talks and individual and group counseling in dormitories. Officials in cooperation with those of other church colleges solicited state industries for the Kansas Foundation for Private Colleges, Inc., whose purpose was "to promote and direct unified approaches to corporations and other organizations for financial support for church-related colleges."[29] The school more and more became a community center for mobile health services, regional disaster and relief groups, annual community occasions, and specialized workshops and conferences.

A world literature class, under the instruction of Mary Miller, reading Greek plays written 500 years before Christ was born.

Academic and curricular developments included those already traced—the acceptance of the high school department into the NCA, aligning the program with the traditional 8-4-2 educational pattern; and a number of others: the addition of more night courses, more extension courses, and a standard program of correspondence courses through materials secured from the University of Nebraska; the discontinuance of spring terms for elementary teachers because of the new state laws requiring training above the junior college level; more sabbatical years; and supported leaves of absence for further study. A change in the nursing affiliation program was necessitated by the closing of the La Junta Mennonite School of Nursing on September 1, 1957. Until affiliation with another Mennonite-operated school of nursing could be secured, the pre-nursing students since the spring of 1956 enrolled for training at the General Hospital School of Nursing at Kansas City, Missouri,[30] which holds accreditation from the National League of Nursing.

Following educational trends, and curriculum revisions by the various departments, the college enlarged its course offerings. Arrangements were made for more piano and voice lessons; evening and day art classes; a driver education course; new counseling courses—marriage and family relations, pastoral counseling, orientation; varied crafts, home arts, and shop courses; a standard business education program in both high school and college; during 1956-57 a reading clinic for both college and high school students.

Field trips became more frequent, extended, and purposeful. Science classes were taken to demonstrations, industries, and local service stations; agriculture classes to study the dairy plan at the State Agricultural College at Manhattan; government classes to observe the state legislature in session; psychology classes to observe and help at mental hospitals and children's homes. The music department annually participated in the district music festivals and gave public voice and piano recitals. Bible classes visited other religious groups—Jewish, Catholic. State and national measurement tests, audio-visual aids, art displays, participation in regional contests—all became a regular part of the program. By faculty action, field trips replaced educational tours in 1958-59.

One of the more aggressive movements of the new administration was an attempt to develop the junior college into a four-year liberal arts college. The idea originated outside the school. The South Central Conference in 1953 passed recommendations

> that the conference continue to give its prayers, moral and active support to those responsible in launching a four-year college program at Hesston;

171

that we as a conference have representatives available for
further study and cooperation with the college administration
and with the Mennonite Board of Education in the continu-
ation and implementation of the program.[31]

By approval of the Educational Policy Committee of the
Mennonite Board of Education a committee consisting of the
dean, the director of public relations, and a conference representative was appointed to study the need and possibility of
establishing a four-year college. Responses to investigation
tended to show that the constituency had increased in numbers,
more young people were attending college, a greater proportion of them were going to non-Mennonite colleges as there
was no (Old) Mennonite four-year college west of the Mississippi River, parents and conference leaders preferred a closer
college, and the demand for college-trained people was increasing. The need seemed evident. Was the change a possibility?
For a four-year college the state required additional training
for teachers, the offering of majors in six to eight departments
meeting University of Kansas requirements, a new dormitory,
additions to the library, and a constituency assuring continued
financial support.[32]

Hopes and questions had been awakened. Help came from
the Study Commission on Mennonite Higher Education. The
Commission appointed a research committee of three members,
one from each of the three (Old) Mennonite colleges—Paul
Bender, Ira E. Miller, and Leonard L. Lichti—to launch a study
of collegiate needs in the Mennonite Church. The theme of
the 1954 annual Businessmen's Banquet was "Hesston Advancing to a Four-Year College." Editorials in the school paper promoted the idea.

The need to change colleges after two years demanded new
adjustments . . . a disruption. A student was geared to contrib-

172

The Choral Union, under the direction of Paul M. Yoder, singing
Handel's THE MESSIAH in December, 1956.

uting after one year; he had become a part of the school.
It was inefficient to send students west of the Mississippi to
two overcrowded schools east of it.[33]

The president wrote:

> It seems clear to me, that as far as the future of Hesston is
> concerned, the alternatives are about three: first, to confine
> ourselves to high school offerings only; second, to continue
> as a high school and junior college; and third, to launch into
> a four-year liberal arts program.
>
> . . . I am wondering what the future holds for the private
> junior college. The community junior college makes sense
> because it gets its enrollment close home. The student simply
> continues his education while he lives at home. But a private
> junior college gets its enrollment from twenty-five states, and
> the large majority . . . are boarding students. . . . Not many
> students will prefer to attend two schools to complete their
> studies.[34]

In the spring of 1956 a curriculum specialist, J. H. Russel
from the University of Denver, was called in to study the Hesston College program and to discover developments essential for
a four-year college. His recommendations included the coordination of the public relations activities of Hesston and Goshen,
the two schools under the same Board; a study of probable
cooperative efforts to avoid duplication; the study of a probable
two-year terminal program for Hesston. The increasing number of Mennonite high schools, the uncertainty of securing required funds, and the scarcity of advanced degrees among the
faculty he thought discouraging to the establishment of a four-
year college.[35]

At the meeting following his report the faculty voted that
the Executive Committee of the Mennonite Board of Education with a committee of employed consultants be asked to
study the wisest move for Hesston College. Should the school
become a four-year college, remain a junior college, or coordinate its program more closely with Goshen College?[36]

In 1956 the Executive Committee of the Mennonite Board of Education assigned a review of the entire problem to the Study Commission on Mennonite Higher Education—John R. Mumaw, president of Eastern Mennonite College, chairman; Paul Mininger, president of Goshen College; Roy D. Roth, president of Hesston College; Paul Erb, editor of the *Gospel Herald;* and Noah Good, principal of Lancaster Mennonite School. The Commission employed two consultants to work with them—Donald M. Mackenzie, Associate Secretary, Commission on Colleges and Universities, North Central Association of Colleges and Secondary Schools; and Gould Wickey, Executive Secretary of the Board of Higher Education, United Lutheran Church in America. After the study and a visit by the consultants to both campuses in the spring of 1957, they issued their findings and recommendations. Among them were these: Hesston College should remain a junior college at least until 1960 and should prepare to make application for the accreditation of the junior college department by the North Central Association of Colleges and Secondary Schools; three new buildings are needed—a men's residence hall, a library, and a fine arts-classroom building; more teachers should have advanced degrees; the B.R.E. (Bachelor of Religious Education) program should be discontinued as it attracts very few students; the presence of the high school makes it difficult to maintain a college program of high quality.

A number of advances followed these studies. In January, 1957, the Hesston College administration met with the president and dean of Goshen College, who agreed, "for the time being to allow the transfer of up to 75 hours of college credit from Hesston to Goshen."[37] During the 1957-58 term the faculty conducted a self-study to retain state accreditation for the junior college, organized an in-service study of the text,

175

Toward a Christian Philosophy of Higher Education, by Gru-
eningen, and investigated with the local school board and local parents the advisability of discontinuing the high school.
Early in 1958, Paul Bender, as an employee of the Executive Committee of the Mennonite Board of Education and a
consultant "to advise Hesston College on its educational program and to study the coordination of Hesston and Goshen,"
arranged with the two administrations that Hesston students
planning to enter the Goshen College Biblical Seminary could
take three full years of Bible training at Hesston. A three-year
program in elementary education was planned for 1959-60, and
a terminal program in industrial arts was arranged. Because
of the educational trends resulting from the scientific advances
in 1958, the high school curriculum was revised to stress liberal
arts courses and to limit electives.

Paul Bender, the consultant employed by the Executive
Committee of the Mennonite Board of Education, had long
acquaintance with Hesston College. As a student and teacher
he was with the school during almost the entire twenty-one
years of the D. H. Bender administration and is the son of
the first president. Most of the years since 1933 he spent
at Goshen College as registrar and teacher. As an appointee
"to study the coordination of Hesston and Goshen," probably
no individual was better fitted.

In 1956 by recommendation of the faculty and action of the
Board, "Hesston College" instead of "Hesston College and
Bible School" became the official name of the school. The
change was made

> to eliminate the possibility of a common misunderstanding
> concerning the kind of institution operated at Hesston, par-
> ticularly on the part of persons who in the past reviewed cer-
> tain official correspondence and statements of credit transfer
> and associated the former name with a Bible institute type of
> school rather than with a liberal arts college.[38]

The J. D. Charles Hall of Science and Arts.

Building needs of the college had been largely supplied by the two major buildings—Hess Hall and Charles Hall— erected in the years just preceding the Roth administration. The J. D. Charles Hall of Science and Arts was finished and dedicated during this administration on February 1, 1952, with the following program:

Open House with Classes in Progress   1:00-4:00 p.m.
Varsity-Alumni Basketball game   4:00-5:00 p.m.
Lunch   5:15 p.m.
Program   7:30 p.m.
    Chairman—President-elect Roth
    Devotions—Maurice A. Yoder
Speeches: What This Building Means
    a. To the Science Department   Vincent J. Krabill
    b. To the Agriculture Department   Lester Culp
    c. To the Music Department   John P. Duerksen
    d. To the Total Educational Program
                                     Dean Walter E. Oswald
Tribute to J. D. Charles and Glenn L. Hershberger
                                              D. D. Driver
Comments   Daniel E. Kauffman
Dedicatory Address   Milo Kauffman
Official Act of Dedication and Prayer
                          Nelson E. Kauffman, President
                             Mennonite Board of Education
Dedicatory Offering in charge of Harry A. Diener
                                  Vice-president of Board
Benediction   Dr. Fred S. Brenneman

177

One page of the program pamphlet was a reprint of dedicatory inscriptions in the new building.

Text of Memorial Bronze Plaque placed in Lobby of Charles Hall:

THIS BUILDING IS DEDICATED TO THE MEMORY OF J. D. CHARLES (1878-1923)

who served Hesston College from the time of its founding until his death fourteen years later. He is remembered especially for thorough scholarship and inspired teaching in the natural sciences. He also rendered outstanding service as an instructor in other fields, as dean and registrar of the college, as pastor of the local congregation, and as author of a number of books and pamphlets. Force of intellect and character gave him profound influence among his colleagues and the students, who revered him as a true educator and a devout Christian. The radiance of his spirit is reflected in these, his own words:

"Let nothing shake your confidence in God, in the Bible, and Jesus your Savior. Let us await calmly and hopefully the great illumination, when all the vain speculations and conceits of men shall be dissipated in the clear, warm light of the Eternal Day of our Lord."

Text of Memorial Bronze Plaque placed in the Physics and Mathematics Room of Charles Hall:

THIS ROOM IS DEDICATED TO THE MEMORY OF GLENN L. HERSHBERGER, 1921-1949

who was taken from this life while teaching an algebra class in the fourth year of his service as instructor in physical science and mathematics. He walked humbly with God and contributed to the life and tradition of Hesston College by the force of his straightforward and sincere Christian character. In appreciation of his purity of purpose and high sense of responsibility, friends and relatives have furnished and equipped this physics classroom and laboratory.

Plans for a new church had been begun in 1947. The location of the building had entailed long discussions and painful compromises. The architect in his plans had placed the building on the front campus, in a location which necessitated the

A view of the south side of the Church-Chapel,
during construction.

destruction of the half-moon drive lined with the cedars which
had for almost half a century been one of the chief attractions
of the campus. So late as April of 1953 the administration
was still discussing the discretion of starting a major building
on the front campus.[39]

But the location of the building had finally been decided.
The local congregation felt an urgent need for more room and
had funds available to complete the Sunday school wing of the
planned building. The college prepared to begin its part of
the construction in 1955.

In June, 1953, the first carload of lumber for the building
was unloaded and the ground-breaking service was held on
Sunday, June 14.[40] By August, construction had progressed to

> running concrete for the basement. The educational or Sun-
> day school wing, now under construction, is the responsibility
> of the Hesston congregation and will probably be completed
> before the new year. The sanctuary proper will be the con-
> joint responsibility of the congregation and the college; and
> the Bible wing, the responsibility of the college.[41]

179

The Church-Chapel Building.

After the Sunday school wing had been finished, construction stopped. In April, 1955, it was reported that "construction of the new church-chapel is to be resumed .... Chapel and BRE annex yet to be built."[42] Work on the building was begun in July, 1955, and progressed so rapidly that by January, 1956, plans "to finish for dedication by commencement" were put into operation.[43] The college goal for the students and faculty spring workdays program was $8,000 to be used to purchase church and classroom furniture.[44] The income exceeded the goal by almost $2,000, the furnishings arrived May 4, installation was completed by May 9, the first service was held in the new church on May 13, and the dedicatory service at 2:00 p.m. on May 27, 1956, with the following program:

Service of Dedication

Chairman	Ivan R. Lind, pastor
Song Leader	Lowell J. Byler, music director
Invocation	Harold Sommerfeld, deacon and chairman of church council
Hymn	Faith of Our Fathers
Devotions	Nelson E. Kauffman, president Mennonite Board of Education
Anthem, Come Unto Him—Handel	Collegiate Chorale
Recognitions	Harry Weaver, chairman Building Committee

Greetings from Former Pastors:
  J. D. Charles (deceased)
  Noah Oyer (deceased)
  D. H. Bender (deceased)
  I. E. Burkhart, Goshen, Indiana
  Milo Kauffman, Hesston, Kansas
  Jess Kauffman, Colorado Springs, Colorado
  J. P. Duerksen, Enkenbach-Pfalz, Germany

Hymn	I Love Thy Kingdom, Lord
Litany of Dedication	
Prayer of Dedication	Roy D. Roth, president Hesston College
Anthem, Founded on Thee—Arr. by Samuel Dyer	
	Collegiate Chorale

Dedicatory Sermon	The Zeal of Thine House
	E. M. Yost, moderator
	South Central Conference
Hymn	Forth In Thy Name, O Lord
Benediction	Milo Kauffman
	Kansas area overseer

Since May, 1956, the daily chapel service has been held in the new church-chapel. The silence as worshippers come and go has heightened the meaning of the moments spent there. Many students have testified that daily chapel is a significant factor in promoting spiritual growth. The prayer room in the new building was furnished by I. Mark Ross, an alumnus and former staff member, and dedicated to his wife, the late Eliza Brenneman Ross. The total cost of the building was $183,334.[45]

A daily chapel service in the Church-Chapel Building.

The contractor, Frank Roupp, who had constructed all the major campus buildings except Green Gables, died on May 13, the day the first church service was held in the new building. Funeral services were held at 2:30 p.m. on May 16, in the building his workmen had just completed.[46]

The annual workdays program, three school days in which students, faculty, and staff worked for friends or business firms in their home communities and gave the profit to the college, had since its beginning in 1950 been an effective business enterprise and morale builder. The first two years after its beginning, its proceeds added almost $12,000 to the Charles Hall fund; from 1952 to 1954 almost $23,000 for operating expenses and shop construction and equipment; in 1955 and 1956 over $16,000 for church-chapel construction and furniture; and in 1957 and 1958 over $43,889 to the men's dormitory fund. During the first nine years the workdays proceeds amounted to $94,738.48.

There were other campus improvements during these years. A 50' x 100' quonset building was added west of the Industrial Arts Shop to house campus maintenance equipment and to serve the agriculture department and metal work activities.[47]

Two houses were purchased for faculty homes.[48] The Mennonite Board of Education approved discontinuing the operation of the Hesston College farm. With student help a sale was arranged for June 1, 1956, to sell livestock and operating equipment and a part of the farm machinery. The proceeds from the sale were added to the 1956 general operating fund. The land was rented for the raising of wheat and other cash crops.[49] The farmhouse became a boys' rooming house.

The dining room and kitchen floors and the floors of several Green Gables rooms were tiled and the home economics department enlarged. The snackshop was redecorated by Bill Garrett, a former art instructor, and named "The Lark's Nest." The road encircling the college became a one-way drive; and campus parking areas were constructed north of Green Gables, behind the Administration Building, and south of the Church and Hess Hall. The picturesque but rather unserviceable cobblestone walk between Green Gables and the Administration Building was covered with asphalt donated by C. A. Brilhart of Scottdale, Pennsylvania.[50] The library was enlarged and a bulletin board and museum display cases were installed in Charles Hall. The old chapel hall in the Administration Building was remodeled into a high school reading room and the "Y room" into a suite of offices for the deans of personnel.

Green Gables and the asphalt walk in the sunshine.

By the spring of 1956 the crowded, unattractive conditions in the boys' rooming houses and the lowered morale resulting from them seemed to make acute the need for a new dormitory for men. By March the Board had given approval to begin plans for a men's dormitory, a committee had been chosen to study dormitory plans, to secure an architect and consult a landscape specialist. To promote and hasten the movement for a new dormitory the men students on December 12, 1956, staged

184

an "Operation Starvation." They ate no meals in the college dining room that day, gave the dollar per person refund from the college to the dormitory fund, and planned to repeat the "operation" often enough to contribute during the year $10 each to the fund. Later the girls too became inspirited with the idea. Friends of the school added to the fund.

A faculty planning committee had since 1956 been visiting modern dormitories and studying plans. In February, 1957, the City Council and other community representatives met with the college administration to review the master campus layout planned by English, Miller, and Hockett, the architects and engineers from Hutchinson, Kansas, who had planned the church-chapel building. In January, 1958, the faculty planning committee recommended that "campus housing be planned for one area, that a new women's dormitory . . . eventually be built on a site adjoining the men's dormitory, with a student union between."[51]

In the president's memo to the faculty on May 16, 1958, the business manager included the following note:

> We have asked the Mennonite Board of Education to approve ground breaking and construction of the men's dormitory, beginning in August or September, 1958. Finances are to be supplied as follows:
>
> | | |
> |---|---|
> | Cash and pledges by July 1, 1958 | $50,000 |
> | Alumni drive by July 1, 1959 | $50,000 |
> | Solicitation in 1958-59 | $50,000 |
>
> Balance to be provided by Board of Education funds. Total proposed cost without furnishings is $300,000. We believe with good management . . . we can also furnish the building for this figure.

When the 1958 workdays goal was being set, an anonymous donor agreed to match students' earnings with any sum not exceeding $15,000. The total workdays figure rose to almost $36,000 and, as previously stated, was added to the dormitory

College library reading room.

fund. At the annual 1958 alumni business meeting during the commencement season, the alumni organization, as a fifty-year anniversary project, decided to raise the $50,000 yet required by the Board before construction could begin. A volunteer fund-raising committee with James Hershberger as chairman was organized to promote the project. In August, 1958, thirty-five area coordinators were called to the campus; and detailed plans were outlined for getting in contact with every alumnus, personally if possible. In eight graduating classes 100 per cent of the members contributed to the fund; and by December, 1958, over $54,000 in cash and pledges had come in from more than 50 per cent of the 2,200 Hesston alumni.

Plans required for the construction of the dormitory were ready and on Friday afternoon, November 28, 1958, during the Thanksgiving weekend, the ground-breaking service occurred. At the program in Hess Hall preceding the actual ground breaking, President Roth presided and the large audience sang

President Roth breaking ground for the new men's dormitory,
November 28, 1958.

praises to God. The previous planning and labors for the new
dormitory and the early future developments were clarified.
President Roth with a gold-painted shovel led the ground-
breaking ceremony. President-elect Tilman R. Smith followed,
and after him seven other representative persons participated.

187

The actual construction began in January, 1959, with John Reschly, of Mt. Pleasant, Iowa, as the builder.

Throughout the years the institution had been continuing its original policy of operating within its income and ceasing construction activities when funds were depleted. The year 1950-51 had closed with a net gain of $159.27, but the next year with a net loss of $382.35, and by 1952-53, budget trouble grew more critical. In March, 1953, the administration reminded the faculty that Board policy required the college to operate within available income even though allowances needed to be cut.[52] As a result, the faculty voted upon themselves a reduction in salaries; and the president-elect to prevent the decrease, sent out letters soliciting funds. Before the close of the term, $6,000 had been sent in response to President-elect Roth's letters; and teachers continued receiving their customary allowances.

Operating expenses rose steadily through the years, from approximately $158,000 in 1950-51 to $228,000 in 1954-55.[53] After the two-year fund drive for the building of Charles Hall was finished, a bolder, more extensive one began in 1953, the three-year Development Program. Since the end of World War II, surveys had been made and needs studied to discover ways in which the Hesston College program could be made more effective and substantial.

As a result of the surveys, more counselors, teachers, and supervisors were employed; and consequently, more funds were needed. The operating expenses of the institution could no longer be met by Church School Day offerings, student fees, and profits from auxiliary enterprises. To meet the expenses of the added services, $25,000 to $30,000 more was needed annually for operating expenses. To secure the needed funds the three-year Hesston College Development Program was planned to extend from October, 1953, to February, 1956, and to bring in $60,000 annually or a total of $180,000. Of the accruing funds, $75,000 was to be used for operating expenses, $80,000 for the college share of the church-chapel building, and $25,000 for remodeling the Administration Building.[54] The old chapel hall was converted into a high school reading room and personnel offices.

The plan provided for a graded system of investment shares extending through the three years and enabled donors to subscribe in proportion to their means. Early responses to the plan were encouraging. In the first three months $16,000 came in, by May $44,000, and by the end of the first year the annual goal had almost been reached.[55] One Iowa farmer raised 1,000 chickens and donated all the profit.[56]

Stimulation was necessary in the second year. In May "the program was $22,000 short."[57] A new field secretary, George H. Beare, was employed.[58] To give the drive impetus, monthly progress reports were made to the constituency and added suggestions outlined for completing the program. In spite of injected stimuli, the plan in January of the last year was still $43,000 short of its goal.[59] The program was then extended to August 24, 1956, and ended with gifts amounting to a total of $170,346, funds sufficient to meet the outlined expenditures. The giving of the constituency was almost doubled during this three-year period.

By April, 1956, a fresh idea for fund-raising was being formulated. The Study Commission on Mennonite Higher Education had asked each college faculty to make a study of inter-related problems regarding the future expansion of the Mennonite higher education program. The study at Hesston College was made on the assumption that the institution would within a few years become a four-year college. From the projected plans the business manager calculated that it would require $13 per member per year from the entire constituency to carry on such a program. Later as a result of the counsel of employed education consultants and study committees, college officials modified the plans to fit junior college needs; and the figure required for the college program was reduced from $13 to $10 per member per year.

Long-tenure instructors. By the end of the 1958-59 school term D. D. Driver had taught 35 years; Maurice A. Yoder 30 years; Milo Kauffman 27 years; and Mary Miller 24 years. Ivan R. Lind, in 1958 after 18 years of service, took up a pastorate in Milford, Nebraska.

Early in 1956, as a result of the integrated planned giving program which Milo Kauffman had advocated in his book, *The Challenge of Christian Stewardship*, Daniel E. Kauffman had been urging various church leaders to consider promoting a unified church finance plan. The program he suggested was a plan to outline all church needs and the funds required for them, and to help congregations discover how they could budget their giving and allocate funds for the combined church needs from a general treasury. Church leaders saw the possibilities of the plan. If the program were to be accepted and implemented by the church conferences, house-to-house solicitation would become unnecessary.[60]

During the summer of 1956 the president of the Board and the president and business manager of the college visited all the conferences of the constituency in the United States and Canada. Prepared charts helped to clarify the over-all needs of the church and the possibility of maintaining a general treasury to meet the various needs.

By the fall of 1957, Mennonite General Conference had adopted a recommendation "to encourage planned and coordinated giving to the support of the Lord's work." Daniel E. Kauffman had in the spring of 1957 received an M.A. degree in college and university financing from Columbia University. As a part of his study he had clarified and refined the integrated giving project and had organized plans for workshops available to all congregations. During the 1957-58 school year he gave a large part of his time to introducing the program to congregations in the constituency. The Mennonite Board of Missions and Charities had appointed Milo Kauffman to accompany him during the summer of 1957 as its representative. Of the new plan of giving Paul E. Mininger, president of Goshen College, wrote:

> The proposal of Hesston College to help congregations face their total financial obligations to all aspects of the church program is the most significant development in church financing in our brotherhood during the past fifty years.[61]

The regular term enrollments during the administration fluctuated—297 in 1951-52; 312 in 1952-53; 269 in 1956-57;

247 in 1957-58. The graduating classes in 1953 totalled 108, the largest in the history of the school. Fewer high school students came because of the increasing number of local Mennonite high schools, and because boarding freshmen and sophomores were no longer encouraged to come. More college students enrolled—111 in 1951-52, 133 in 1956-57, 146 in 1958-59. Spring terms as mentioned previously were discontinued after 1952-53 since they no longer furthered the certification of teachers. Winter Bible Term enrollments dwindled from 56 in 1950-51 to 9 in 1955-56;[62] and thereafter the six weeks Special Bible Terms were discontinued. In 1957-58 there were 77 second-generation alumni (children of alumni) enrolled and three from the third generation (grandchildren), 31.2% of the student body.[63]

Student activities during these years were not unlike those of

Students returning from chapel.

previous administrations. The group continued "going over the top" in goals set by all-school organizations—in workdays and Y drives. The Y surveyed needy white and colored sections of nearby cities to establish regular teaching stations. Gospel teams were sent out annually; during the summer of 1954 one team visited eighty churches south and west of Kansas; and in 1957 President Roth and the Collegiate Men's Quartet spent the entire summer visiting churches in the West. As in previous years the Y experimented with street meetings in surrounding cities and in prison and rescue mission services, helped in reconstruction work in the Arkansas flood areas, held annual drives to raise funds for various mission and charitable purposes, and in 1953 sponsored its first radio evangelism program, "Christ for You," with Elam Hollinger, a student minister, as the speaker, and the Evangelaires, a men's quartet, accompanying him.[64]

Although participation in extramural forensic activities was limited, students continued entering the state anti-alcohol oratorical contests sponsored annually by the Women's Christian Temperance Union. Dellis Schrock won second place in 1951, Willard Roth third in 1953, Melvin Schmidt first in the state and third in the national in 1956, Dean Byers second in the state in 1958. The first Forensics Council to coordinate student speech activities on and off campus was organized in 1956-57, under the direction of Wandalee Weaver, instructor in college freshman English. Students participated in the anti-alcohol and peace contests off campus and in intercollegiate poetry reading contests,[65] and gave at least one major play annually.

The clubs were largely extensions of the more practical courses—Industrial Arts Club, Home Arts, Nurses', Agriculture, Fishermen's. The Education Club became in 1956 the

Pestalozzi Chapter of the Future Teachers of America. The Audubon Club continued. The Expression Club from 1953 to 1956 gave two plays annually instead of the traditional Christmas play, whose cast was thereafter chosen from the all-school group. After 1956-57 the Forensics Council replaced the Expression Club. In 1954-55 and again in 1957-58 and in 1958-59 an Astronomy Club was active, and in 1956-57 a Business Club and a Shakespeare Society.

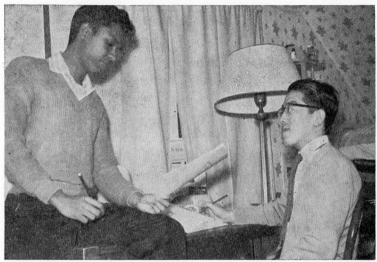

Students from Java and Japan, Subijantoro Atmosuwito and Junji Yamamoto.

In 1952-53, eighty-eight students were doing part-time work for the institution. There were seven students from other lands on the campus—five of them from Puerto Rico. One school dinner during the year was an outdoor Puerto Rican pig roast.[66] In 1954-55 one high school senior, Ellen Penner, won the highest score of the 13,811 Kansas seniors who took the comprehensive tests. In 1956 the bookkeeping class taught by Miss Ellen M. Miller won first place in the Private Schools and

Colleges Division of the International Bookkeeping Contest sponsored by Gregg-McGraw-Hill.[67]

In 1951-52 the Student Council as the official representative body of the students of Hesston College

> recommended to the administration that the traditional citizenship award annually presented to the one outstanding citizen of Hesston College and Bible School be permanently discontinued, inasmuch as it is currently considered that such an award is not consistent with the fundamental principles of Christ-like living which our school has tried to maintain.[68]

The recommendation was accepted and citizenship awards discontinued. The Student Council had grown more active in recent years, planning all-school socials, dress-up suppers, other physical and cultural advances for dormitories, dining room, and student gatherings.

In 1952-53 the assistant maintenance man, Charles Greaser, known to many students as "Uncle Charley," fell from the steel framework of the new shop extension and fractured several bones. In the early morning of March 10, 1955, a fire started in the milk house and was noticed almost simultaneously by two late-working professors who called in both the Hesston and Newton fire departments. The fire was under control almost immediately and the event became a social one as the college men and women had turned out *en masse*. In the spring of 1958 a student, Gordon Hershberger, was critically injured in a baseball game.

During recent years new scholarship funds have been started. Oregon friends of the school started a fund for colored students. To honor the late Jacob and Barbara Brenneman for their interest in education and missions, their son, Dr. Fred S. Brenneman, and Mrs. Brenneman established a fund to help worthy students prepare for full-time church service. Other funds have been started by Mr. and Mrs. E. B. Harder of Up-

195

land, California; H. N. Kulp of Filer, Idaho; Yoder Feeds, Inc., Kalona, Iowa; the Eliza Brenneman Ross Memorial Grant; and the Schowalter Foundation, Inc., Newton, Kansas. The Menno Shellenberger Memorial and the Ruth Diener Grants had been established previously. From the Schowalter Foundation, Inc., the college began to receive substantial grants annually, as much as $7,000 in 1957.

In 1955-56 fifty-one German art masterpieces by contemporary artists were presented to the Mennonite Central Committee by Theodore Heuss, president of the Federal Republic of Germany, as a thank-you gift of the German people to the Mennonites of America for their assistance during the years of Germany's recovery from the war. These were on display at Hesston College from November 16 to 26, 1955.

On May 2, 1957, President Roth presented his resignation to the Executive Committee of the Mennonite Board of Education, to become effective on June 2, 1958. The Board began a search for a new president, but by the spring of 1958 it had found none. *This Month* of March, 1958, stated that

> Roy D. Roth, who has resigned as president of Hesston College, has accepted the request of the Mennonite Board of Education Executive Committee to continue to serve as president for the 1958-59 school year.

On October 23, 1958, the Mennonite Board of Education at its annual business meeting at Kidron, Ohio, elected Tilman R. Smith of Eureka, Illinois, as the fourth president of Hesston College, to take office on July 1, 1959.

The president-elect had attended the academy of Hesston College for four years, 1919-23; had received the B. A. degree from Goshen College in 1928; the M.A. degree in social studies from the University of Iowa; the M.S. degree in school administration from the University of Illinois. For nineteen years he had served the Roanoke High School in Illinois, four years as instructor and fifteen years as superintendent-principal. For ten years, 1949-59, he was superintendent of the Eureka Community School District in Illinois.

The years of the Roth administration were not smooth, easy ones. The pillar of cloud grew indistinct and "tarried." The constituency suffered years of drought and crop failures while living costs rose and student fees were increased. There were good free high schools available in home communities, and more and more Mennonite high schools were started in localities where many Mennonite families lived. High school enrollment gradually decreased from 173 in 1952-53 to 104 in 1958-59. The pressures and dissatisfaction of the more liberal segment of the constituency on the one hand conflicted with those of the more conservative segment on the other. Because of the era of general change in Mennonite Church thought and discipline, the difficulties were intensified.

President Roth during the years of his administration gave himself unstintingly to advance the institution. In public address he was sensitive, dignified, effective—trusted by faculty and students alike to perform official communications graciously. He spent long hours overtime organizing, arranging, that plans and activities might proceed smoothly and effectively. The summer months and many school days and weekends he spent in visiting conferences and congregations to effect closer unity and interests between the school and the constituency. During the year, 1956-57, he and Kenneth E. King, the acting business manager, visited congregations three out of four weekends during the entire school year. In the years of his administration he won the confidence and good will of the friends of the school. The president spoke at commencement exercises of grade schools, high schools, and colleges; he addressed various high school and college educational meetings; and in 1956 he was elected the secretary-treasurer of the Kansas Council of Church-Related Colleges. He taught extension Bible classes; spoke frequently in other Mennonite circles, even for evangelistic meetings; and spent a great deal of time away from the campus in various types of meetings and conferences throughout the midwestern United States and the Mennonite areas in Canada.

To promote a genial, family-type fellowship among students, faculty, parents, and friends, President and Mrs. Roth maintained a practically continuous open house. On Friday and Sunday evenings the president's home was open to students who wished to come. Each spring President and Mrs. Roth invited all the dormitory men to a hamburger or chicken fry on their lawn. In their home they held a reception for graduates and their parents at commencement time. As a part of the fall orientation program, the president inaugurated a reception for students, parents, and faculty. During the Christmas season President and Mrs. Roth entertained in their home the administrative officers and their wives and at other times the personnel staff. From his personal funds he subsidized the cost of the faculty fall retreat at Rocky Mountain Camp in 1956.

Like his home, his office and time were open to callers. Students came for counsel early and late, even on Sundays. Teachers came to discuss problems. In case of illness or accident within the school group, the president was one of the first and most frequent visitors. He spent time in the boys' dormitories, frequently conducted student prayer meetings and taught their Sunday school classes. When active arrangements for a men's dormitory were begun, the president visited each of the boys' rooming houses, showed them the tentative plans and stirred

Commencement on the East Lawn, June 2, 1958.

their interest in helping increase the fund. Together they
planned "Operation Starvation," a project previously described
in this chapter.

Academically, too, the president inaugurated a number of
advances. Overdue sabbatical leaves were arranged; a degree
assistance program was planned and put into operation to encourage further graduate work. For those teachers studying
for doctoral degrees, tuition and $125 per month for living ex-
penses were paid. During the years of the Roth administration, seventeen faculty members secured advanced degrees.
On the faculty in 1959 were two with the doctor's degree, one
with the specialist's degree, and three more who had nearly
fulfilled requirements for the doctoral degree.

Other faculty services were inaugurated during President
Roth's administration. There were substantial increases in
teachers' salaries. The faculty allowance schedule was revised
to give each teacher and official the same basic salary with differences made for number of dependents, number of months of
employment, and special responsibilities. An organized effort
was made to help teachers find summer employment cor-
responding to their training.

Concerning the responsibility and nature of the teacher's
mission President Roth wrote in "The President's Message" in
the 1957-1959 Hesston College Catalog:

> We need teachers who can give quality instruction. For
> while the Christian educator is first of all a Christian, he is al-
> ways an educator. He is a man with a keen, active mind, and
> with a capacity for hard work. He is not slipshod in method
> or desultory in procedure. He is a master of the knowledge
> in his specialty. He stays abreast the progress and develop-
> ments in his field and keeps on the lookout for whatever ap-
> proaches and innovations will improve his performance. He
> is unafraid of change and welcomes opportunities for experi-
> mentation. He is dissatisfied with the present, but is always
> optimistic about the future. He thinks of his work as a min-

istry to the human intellect and spirit. He grows in his profession because he is a thinker and a philosopher. He increases in stature as a teacher because he respects the personality of youth and rejoices in the advancement and progress of each new generation.

Students, faculty, and constituency recognized that the president's over-all interest was a spiritual one. Each Monday morning in chapel he gave searching devotional talks that spoke to the hearts of students and affected their thinking and living. At the time and afterward students often spoke of the Monday morning chapel talks in active appreciation and often sought the president to conduct other student meetings. During the revival meetings held annually on the campus President Roth arranged for special periods of the day to be set aside for prayer, Bible reading, and meditation. He encouraged maintaining a spiritual tone in classes, in social gatherings, in dormitory living, and in daily relationships. Faculty and stu-

Green Gables, fifty years later, 1959.

dents alike were always conscious of an active spiritual motivation.

In spite of the discouraging elements already related, endeavor and spirit on the campus remained strong during this administration. A letter from a member of the inspection team that came in the spring of 1958 to check the institution for reaccreditation by state agencies had a ring reminiscent of the fervor of the founders of the school.

> Dear President Roth:
>
> This note is to thank you, your faculty, and your student body for the courtesy shown me during the State Department visit to your campus. Never have I been so impressed with the seriousness of purpose, the dedication of lives, and the prevailing Christian spirit that I witnessed at Hesston. The Church and its leaders are to be commended for providing this type of an education for its young people.
>
> Yours truly,
> /S/
> Chairman

Particularly notable for school spirit and spiritual tone was the year 1958-59. Faculty and students were united in an earnestness of purpose and zeal. Institutional morale was high. Visitors to the campus commented about the warmth pervading the school atmosphere. It seemed that the Lord was crowning the fiftieth year of Hesston College with His special benediction and blessing.

This administration, like the previous ones, had sought and planned—and tarried. The studies made and trends predicted evidenced a readiness "to journey onward." The more recent developments betokened the imminence of a new forward movement.

> *And so it was, when the cloud abode from even*
> *unto the morning, and that the cloud was taken up*
> *in the morning, then they journeyed: whether it was*
> *by day or by night that the cloud was taken up, they*
> *journeyed.* —Numbers 9:21

VII. THE PRODUCT

*And all the people saw the cloudy pillar stand at
the tabernacle door: and all the people rose up
and worshipped, every man in his tent door.*
— Exodus 33:10

Time and its inevitable changes and the intangibility of
spirit illumination render impossible any conclusive evaluation
of the contributions of Hesston College. That spiritual and
intellectual energies quickened there have advanced the "lea-
vening of the whole lump" seems quite apparent.

For almost fifty years graduates have been leaving the college—at first in classes of five to twelve, later in numbers of a
hundred and more. In the communities and churches to which
these graduates and non-graduates return they become a central

Hesston Main Street. Practically all the town businesses are
managed by alumni of the college.

part of the staying power that holds and lifts—and **gives**. Trustworthy and unspectacular, they minister in their places— libraries, banks, schools, hospitals, churches, missions. They work in construction gangs on the highways, in **PAX** groups and refugee camps in foreign countries, in post offices, in motels, in government services, in inventors' shops, in doctors' and dentists' offices. They build houses and raise meat, grain, milk, and vegetables. In their places they serve, faithful to the trust life has given them. In the city of Hesston most of the Main Street businesses are operated by ex-college students.

In PAX service in France. Howard Snyder '57.

In the thirty-six states in which the alumni live, in the three provinces of Canada, in European and Asian countries, and in islands of the sea they have established homes in which the seed planted at Hesston College has grown into rich fruit. Fathers and mothers, sturdy in the conviction that life is **more**

In the restaurant. Mildred Swartzendruber Klassen '33 and
Vivian Reil '53.

In the post office. S. N. Nunemaker '12, right, was postmaster
from 1918 to 1952.

than bread-earning, instill in their children a certainty that
the truth which sets them free is worth giving their lives and

205

energies to. These children permeated with like conviction form a large part of the present student body.

In the home. Amy Janzen Hershberger '52.

A sense of responsibility for passing on to others the truth that sets men free is persistent in Hesston College youth. Many alumni and children of alumni are giving their lives to carry the Gospel to those who have not heard. They serve in India, in Africa, Japan, South America, Puerto Rico. Many congregations west of the Mississippi River and a number east of it have ministers and bishops who were once Hesston College students. A 1954 survey revealed that 100 per cent of the advanced Bible alumni were active in church work, 88 per cent of the junior college graduates, and 36 per cent of the high school.[1] In city missions—Cleveland, Chicago, Los Angeles, Pueblo, Detroit, Saginaw, Kansas City, Hannibal, Wichita, Hutchinson—Hesston College alumni are working in the pulpits, in visitation, in kitchens and laundries, in administrative positions, and in maintenance tasks. In rural districts in Missouri, Oklahoma,

Arkansas, Oregon, Canada, Minnesota, Mississippi, New Mexico, Texas, Arizona, and elsewhere are mission stations and outpost Sunday schools in which its former students are teaching the Word and living with the people.

In the schools of the land are many alumni. Each year, almost from the beginning, the college has sent out into elementary schools from ten to twenty-five teachers to nurture the minds and hearts of children into clearer, purer atmospheres. Here and there its graduates have become teachers in high schools and universities. On the faculties and in the administrative offices of the Mennonite church schools, Hesston College graduates are well represented. On the teaching staffs of all three (Old) Mennonite colleges are earlier and later graduates of Hesston College including a president, a president-elect, a registrar, dean of a seminary, and both a long-term former president and dean. Mennonite high schools springing up in later years are often partly staffed by former students of Hesston College.

In the school room. John Zook '51, '53.

In the doctor's office. Dr. Florence Cooprider Friesen '16.

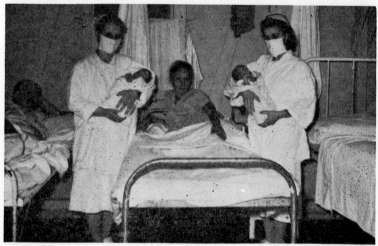

In the hospital. The nurse to the left is Virginia Showalter '44.

The church hospitals west of the Mississippi River are administered almost entirely by Hesston College alumni. The nursing school at the La Junta, Colorado Hospital, which for many years was the only institution serving the church in the training of nurses, was promoted, kept accredited and staffed by Hesston alumni. Annually the college sends into the hospitals from ten to twenty girls to become the kind of nurses who do more than alleviate bodily suffering. Among Hesston alumni are doctors, dentists, nurses, social workers, relief workers who labor where the need is sore, whose extra-mile services awaken to new life the spirits of men.

The alumni of the college are also active in the publishing and writing interests of the church. The editors of the *Gospel Herald, Christian Living, The Mennonite Weekly Review,* and

In the Mennonite Publishing House. Back row, left to right: Mrs. Milford Paul '42; Isla Zink; Elam Hernley; John A Hostetler '45; Millard Lind '40; Laura Showalter; Bertha Nitzsche '28, '31. Front row, left to right: Mrs. Estie Yoder '18; Kathryn Kreider '53; Mrs. John A. Hostetler '45; Mrs. Paul Erb; Freda Hartzler '56. Not on picture, Paul Erb '14.

of a number of local papers were Hesston College students. Many of the contributors to these papers are former students. Many of the books by Mennonite authors were written by Hesston alumni. To the present time all the Conrad Grebel lectures have been given by former students of the college.

Conrad Grebel Lecturers. Top row, left to right: Paul E. Mininger '25, '28, '30; Milo Kauffman '22, '26; Guy F. Hershberger '23. Bottom row, left to right: Paul Erb '14; Gideon G. Yoder '31, '36; Chester K. Lehman '19; J. D. Graber '22.

On the boards and committees of the church the school is well represented. The Mission Board, the Board of Education, the conference boards, the relief services—many of them are headed by Hesston alumni. A large number of these leaders were graduates of those early years, 1918-1927, when Hesston College was giving four years of college work and serving the church at large.

In the Mission Board headquarters. Left to right: J. D. Graber '22; Mrs. J. D. Graber '22; Evelyn Zuercher; Nelson E. Kauffman '25, '29, '31.

Later studies seem to indicate that the loyalty and service of younger alumni equal that of the earlier ones. In 1954 a survey was made of alumni who attended Hesston College during the ten-year period, 1943-53. The purpose of the study was to discover what contribution Hesston alumni were making to the church. Of the 534 persons who answered the questionnaire, there were 24 serving in foreign missions and 104 in city or rural missions; 54 were pastors in America or were wives of pastors; 29 were teaching in church high schools or colleges; 109 were working in the institutional program of the church—hospitals, old people's homes, children's homes, publishing houses; 262 were Sunday school superintendents or teachers; 83.9% of those attending Hesston in this ten-year period were making a direct contribution to the church.

In the front ranks the alumni and former students of Hesston College move with eyes alert for the pillar of cloud that leads on into clearer light. On the home grounds in their own churches and communities they serve and love and lift. In the homes they raise high the Light of trust and instill in young lives the confidence that the Truth indeed will set them free!

In the daytime also he led them with a cloud, and all the night with a light of fire. —Psalm 78:14

In youth work in Puerto Rico. Frederick Springer '52.

On the farm. Allen '37 and Pauline Jantz '39 Diller.

In the print shop. Harold '26, '30 and Ida Hostetler '26, '28 Sommerfeld.

In the Mennonite Central Committee office at Akron, Pennsylvania. Left to right: Merrill Raber '52, Beatrice Brenneman '55, Willard Roth '53, J. N. '21, '24 and Edna Miller '23 Byler.

In the automobile business. Alvin B. King '18, owner; Wilma McFarlane '29 King; Earl Buckwalter; Wilbur Young '47; and Kenneth Hostetler.

In the grocery store. Elmer and Hazel Hoffman '21 '26 Long, managers; and Margaret Long.

215

In the factory. Lyle E. Yost '31, president.

On the India mission field.
Edwin I. Weaver '26; Jacob Flisher, Jr. '45; and S. Paul Miller.

In the bank. R. W. Ruth, '29 cashier; Cecile Stratton '33 Ruth; Mary Catherine Ruth '55; Rebecca Ruth '59; and Marian McFarlane Byler.

"In the heart
of the nation . . ."

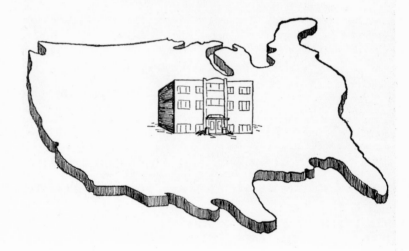

Hesston College Song

In the heart of the nation with faith flaming strong,
    Lives the answer to vision and prayer;
Over age mellowed prairies come strains of a song
    In the fragrant and velvety air;
O, sweet as romance in the whispering night,
    Flows the melody "Truth makes you free."
So haunting, alluring in mystical might
    Comes the call of the College to me.

In the heart of the state on the nurturing sod,
    Hesston College enhances our lore.
And with loyal faith honors and glorifies God,
    With silvery soft, lyric outpour.
The tender and fervent devotion to Christ,
    And submission to Holy decree,
Yield spiritual riches and wisdom unpriced;
    To His glory our College shall be.

In the heart of the tawny and burnished wheat lands,
    Glows the answer to prayer and to dreams,
And the glad sun caresses with soft golden hands
    Where the spirit of holiness gleams.
In my yearning and dreaming unbidden tears start,
    Hesston College is calling to me;
O, dear Alma Mater, enshrined in my heart,
    I pledge my devotion to thee.

—Ursula Miller

The Alma Mater.

PROGRESS INDOMITABLE
1955

Marilyn Kauffman

Paul M. Yoder

With Spirit

The Pep Song.

REFERENCE NOTES
APPENDICES
BIBLIOGRAPHY
INDEX

REFERENCE NOTES

CHAPTER I

[1]Hartzler, J. E., *Education Among the Mennonites of America,* pp. 19-22.
[2]*Ibid.,* p. 31.
[3]Wenger, John C., *Glimpses of Mennonite History,* pp. 6-7.
[4]*Ibid.,* pp. 21-22.
[5]Horsch, John L., *Mennonites in Europe,* Vol. I., p. 300.
[6]*Ibid.,* pp. 301-302.
[7]*Ibid.,* pp. 300-302.
[8]Wenger, *op. cit.,* p. 35.
[9]Hartzler, *op. cit.,* pp. 27-28.
[10]Smith, C. Henry, *The Mennonites of America,* Goshen, Indiana, Published by Author, 1909.
[11]*Ibid.,* pp. 37-38.
[12]Wenger, *op. cit.,* pp. 51-53. Only the organization within the (Old) Mennonite Church is dealt with here and hereafter.
[13]*Gospel Herald,* Jan. 20, 1910, p. 673.
[14]*Christian Monitor,* March, 1910, Editorial page.
[15]Kauffman, Daniel, *The Mennonite Church and Current Issues,* p. 126.
[16]Wenger, S. B., *Gospel Herald,* June 13, 1908, pp. 172-173.
[17]Wenger, S. B., "Complete Organization," *Gospel Witness,* Oct. 28, 1907, p. 407.
[18]Shoemaker, J. S., "Living Issues," *Gospel Witness,* p. 524.
[19]Wenger, Edith, "Why Educate Our Girls?" *Gospel Herald,* July 29, 1909.
[20]"Problems of the Denominational School," reprinted in *Gospel Herald,* p. 12, April 3, 1909, from *Gospel Messenger.*

CHAPTER II

[1]*Gospel Witness,* Oct. 23, 1907, p. 472.
[2]Heatwole, J. A., *Gospel Witness,* Nov. 13, 1907, p. 521.
[3]*Ibid.,* Nov. 13, 1907, p. 526.
[4]Risser, Emma King, daughter of Mrs. S. B. King, Hesston, Kansas, Personal interview.
[5]Kauffman, Daniel, "Issues at Stake," *Gospel Herald,* Aug. 12, 1909, p. 313.
[6]*Gospel Witness,* Nov. 27, 1907, p. 552.
[7]Erb, T. M., Letter, Dec. 2, 1907.
[8]Erb, T. M., Diary.
[9]Erb, T. M., Notebook "History of Hesston Academy and Bible School."
[10]"Board of Education," *Gospel Herald,* July 11, 1908, p. 237.
[11]Erb, T. M., Notebook.
[12]Original copy of ballots.
[13]Erb, T. M., Notebook.
[14]Erb, T. M., Correspondence Files, Oct. 3, 1908.
[15]*Ibid.,* Sept. 1, 1908.
[16]*Ibid.,* Sept. 21, 1908.
[17]*Ibid.,* Nov. 14, 1908.
[18]*Ibid.,* Oct. 5, 1908.
[19]*Ibid.,* Oct. 5, 1908.

[20]*Ibid.,* Sept. 14, 1908.
[21]*Ibid.,* Jan. 6, 1909.
[22]"Report of Mo.-Iowa Conference held Sept. 24, 25," *Gospel Herald,* Oct. 10, 1908, p. 445.
[23]*Gospel Herald,* Nov. 7, 1908, pp. 510-511.
[24]Erb, T. M., Notebook.
[25]Local board minutes.
[26]Erb, T. M., Notebook.
[27]*Ibid.*
[28]Erb, T. M., Correspondence Files, Oct. 3, 1908.
[29]*Ibid.,* Feb. 19, 1909.
[30]*Ibid.,* Oct. 29, 1908.
[31]*Ibid.,* Oct. 28, 1908.
[32]*Ibid.,* Mar. 20, 1909.
[33]*Ibid.,* Nov. 22, 1907.
[34]*Ibid.,* Feb. 10, 1909.
[35]*Ibid.,* Aug. 24, 1908.
[36]*Ibid.,* Dec. 28, 1908.
[37]*Ibid.,* Nov. 14, 1908.
[38]*Ibid.,* Aug. 24, 1908.
[39]*Ibid.,* Dec. 28, 1908.
[40]*Ibid.,* Jan. 14, 1909.
[41]*Ibid.,* Nov. 3, 1908.
[42]*Ibid.,* Nov. 22, 1907.
[43]Erb, T. M., Notebook.
[44]Erb, T. M., Correspondence Files, Jan. 29, 1909.
[45]Erb, T. M., Correspondence Files, Feb. 11, 1909, and Mar. 15, 1909.
[46]Erb, T. M., Notebook.
[47]*Ibid.*
[48]*H. A. and B. S. Bulletins.*
[49]Erb, T. M., Correspondence Files, Jan. 29, 1909.
[50]*Gospel Herald,* Sept. 5, 1908.
[51]*Hesston Academy and Bible School Bulletin,* Announcement for 1909-1910.
[52]*Ibid.*
[53]Local board notes, Sept. 27, 1909.
[54]*Ibid.,* Sept. 27, 1909.
[55]*Ibid.,* Dec. 20, 1909.

CHAPTER III

[1]Erb, T. M., Diary, Sept. 21, 1909.
[2]*Ibid.*
[3]Faculty meeting notes, Sept. 16, 1909.
[4]Erb, T. M., Diary, Sept. 22, 1909.
[5]Faculty meeting notes, Sept. 22, 1909.
[6]Registrar's records.
[7]Erb, T. M., Correspondence files.
[8]Erb, T. M., Diary, Oct. 2, 1909.
[9]*Ibid.*
[10]Bender, D. H., *Gospel Herald,* Dec. 9, 1909, p. 588.
[11]*Ibid.*
[12]*H. A. B. S. Bulletin,* 1911.
[13]Bender, D. H., "Hesston College and Bible School; Its History and Purpose," *H. C. Journal,* Feb., 1919.

[14]Bender, D. H., "Books for Hesston College," *Gospel Herald*, Dec. 29, 1910, p. 626.
[15]"Correspondence," *Gospel Herald*, Oct. 14, 1909, p. 457.
[16]Bender, D. H., *Gospel Herald*, Dec. 9, 1909, p. 588.
[17]Faculty meeting notes, Jan. 17, 1910.
[18]*Ibid.*, May 2, 1910.
[19]Bender, D. H., "Our Financial Story"—a Pamphlet, Feb., 1926.
[20]Bender, D. H., *Gospel Herald*, Dec. 9, 1909, p. 588.
[21]*Gospel Herald*, Oct. 13, 1910, p. 447.
[22]"Report of the Meeting of the Mennonite Board of Education," *Gospel Herald*, May 31, 1910, p. 173.
[23]Local board notes, Mar. 7, 1910.
[24]*Gospel Herald*, Apr. 29, 1910, p. 626.
[25]Principal's and Business Manager's Report for School Year Ending May 31, 1911.
[26]"Correspondence," *Gospel Herald*, May 26, 1910, p. 121.
[27]Principal's and Business Manager's Report for School Year Ending May 31, 1911.
[28]*Ibid.*
[29]Local board notes, June 6, 1911.
[30]*Ibid.*
[31]Principal's and Business Manager's Report for Year Ending, 1913.
[32]*Ibid.*, 1915.
[33]Principal's and Business Manager's Report for Year Ending 1913.
[34]*Christian Monitor*, Dec., 1912, p. 754.
[35]Official notes, p. 7.
[36]Erb, T. M., Diary.
[37]Report, 1913, *op. cit.*
[38]Erb, T. M., Diary, June 3, 1912.
[39]*Ibid.*, June 6, 1912.
[40]Official notes, p. 9.
[41]Erb, T. M., Diary, Nov. 3, 1911.
[42]*Ibid.*, March 22, 1912.
[43]*Ibid.*, April 10, 1912.
[44]Faculty meeting notes, Nov. 4, 1911.
[45]*Ibid.*, Nov. 15, 1911.
[46]Official school notes, p. 6.
[47]*Ibid.*, p. 5.
[48]Bender, D. H., *Bulletin*, "A Bit of History," 1924.
[49]Erb, T. M., Diary, March. 13, 1911.
[50]*Ibid.*, June 1, 1912.
[51]*Ibid.*, June 5, 1912.
[52]Bender, D. H., "Bro. Erb Anointed," *Gospel Herald*, Jan. 23, 1913, p. 683.
[53]Erb, T. M., Diary,
[54]"Correspondence," *Gospel Herald*, Aug. 13, 1914.
[55]Official notes, 1914-15.
[56]"Correspondence," *Gospel Herald*, Oct. 6, 1913.
[57]Erb, T. M., Diary, Mar. 22, 1913.
[58]Bender, D. H., *Lark*, 1923, p. 5.
[59]Erb, T. M., Letter to Kansas Board of Education.
[60]"College Bible Course," *Bulletin*, June, 1928.
[61]"Annual Meeting of the Board of Education," *Gospel Herald*, Sept. 6, 1928, p. 477.
[62]"College Bible Course," *Bulletin*, June, 1928.
[63]"Annual Meeting of Mennonite Board of Education," *Gospel Herald*, Dec. 5, 1929, p. 734.

[64]*H. A. Journal,* Aug.-Sept., 1918, p. 2.
[65]Local board notes, Oct. 9, 1918.
[66]*H. A. Journal,* Nov., 1918, p. 4.
[67]Faculty meeting notes, Apr. 25, 1916.
[68]President's, Dean's and Business Manager's Report for the Year Ending June 10, 1919.
[69]Faculty meeting notes, May 23, 1922.
[70]"Report of Finance Committee of Mennonite Board of Education," *Gospel Herald,* June 3, 1926, p. 207.
[71]*Lark,* 1924.
[72]Erb, Paul, "Hesston College Achievements," *H. C. Journal,* Aug.-Sept., 1925, p. 5.
[73]Erb, T. M., Diary, Jan. 28, 1927.
[74]Bender, D. H., "J. D. Charles Memorial Service," *H. C. Journal,* Oct., 1923.
[75]*Ibid.*
[76]*H. C. Journal,* Aug.-Sept., 1922.
[77]*Ibid.*
[78]*Ibid.*
[79]Bender, D. H., "The Death of J. D. Charles and Its Effect on Hesston College and Bible School," *Gospel Herald,* Sept. 3, 1923.
[80]Bender, D. H., "A Bit of History," *Hesston College and Bible School Bulletin,* 1924.
[81]*H. C. Journal,* Memorial number, Mar., 1929.
[82]Official school notes, p. 20.
[83]*Ibid.,* p. 21.
[84]Official school notes, p. 28.
[85]Local board notes, Feb. 12, 1924.
[86]Charles, J. D., "School Spirit and Student Classification," *H. C. Journal,* Nov., 1919, p. 4.
[87]Charles, J. D., "School Spirit and Student Classification," *Ibid.,* Nov., 1919, p. 4.
[88]Charles, J. D., "Instruction in the Dead Languages," *Ibid.,* Jan., 1919.
[89]Charles, J. D., "The Educational and Cultural Value of Discipline and Government," *Ibid.,* Feb., and Mar., 1923.
[90]*Ibid.,* Jan., 1923.
[91]Eby, Alta Mae, "Economy in the Learning Process," *Ibid.,* Mar., 1916, pp. 10-11.
[92]Yoder, Edward, "The Uses of Adversity," *Ibid.,* Vol. IV, Aug.-Sept., 1917, pp. 8-9.
[93]*Ibid.,* Feb., 1916, p. 8.
[94]Bender, D. H., "Our Financial Story," 1926, Pamphlet.
[95]*H. A. Journal,* Apr., 1916, p. 7.
[96]Erb. T. M., Diary, Feb. 3, 1917.
[97]*H. C. Journal,* May, 1918.
[98]*Ibid.*
[99]*Ibid.,* Aug.-Sept., 1918, p. 2.
[100]Official notes, 1918-19.
[101]*H. C. Journal,* Dec., 1918.
[102]*Ibid.,* Mar., 1919.
[103]*Ibid.,* Feb., 1920, p. 5.
[104]*Ibid.,* Apr., 1920, p. 9.
[105]*Ibid.,* Nov., 1920, p. 4.
[106]Bender, D. H., "Our Financial Story," 1926.
[107]"Endowment Program for Christian Education," Mennonite Board of Education, 1927.
[108]*H. C. Journal,* Mar., 1927, pp. 14-15.

109*Ibid.*, May, 1929.
110*Ibid.*
111*Gospel Herald,* Sept., 6, 1928. "Annual Meeting of Board of Education."
June 1, 2, 4, 1928, p. 477.
112*H. C. Catalog,* 1930-31, p. 23.
113Erb, T. M., Diary, April 23, 1918.

CHAPTER IV

1Letters on file, Aug. 28, 1930.
2The Local Board members now were Maurice A. Yoder, chairman; I. E. Burkhart, Edward Yoder, Earl Buckwalter, C. A. Vogt, C. M. Hostetler, Charles Diener.
3*Lark,* 1931, p. 18.
4Adm. committee notes, Dec. 22, 1930.
5*Ibid.,* Jan. 5, 1931 and April 24, 1931.
6*H. C. Journal,* 1930, p. 13.
7*Ibid.,* Mar. 12, 1931, p. 9.
8*Gospel Herald,* Mar. 12, 1931, p. 1071.
9Adm. committee notes, Dec. 1, 1930.
10*Gospel Herald,* Mar. 12, 1931, p. 1069.
11Official notes, 1931-32, p. 39.
12*H. C. Journal,* Nov., 1931.
13*Ibid.,* Nov., 1931.
14*Gospel Herald,* Nov., 1931.
15*Ibid.*
16Heatwole, J. A., Letter, Oct. 18, 1931.
17Local board notes, May 10, 1932.

CHAPTER V

1Local board notes, July 1, 1932.
2"Report of Meeting of Mennonite Board of Education," *Gospel Herald,* Apr. 21, 1932, p. 61.
3*Ibid.,* June 2, 1932, p. 178.
4Kauffman, Milo. First sermon to Hesston Congregation after his appointment as president.
5Local board notes, July, 1932.
6"Iowa-Nebraska Conference Report," *Gospel Herald,* Oct. 13, 1932, p. 605.
7Local board notes, July 1, 1932.
8Faculty meeting notes, Apr. 11, 1933.
9Kauffman, Milo, "President's Report," Annual Meeting of Mennonite Board of Education, Feb. 6, 7, 1933.
10*Ibid.*
11*Ibid.*
12"Mrs. Erb's Study Suggestions," *H. C. Journal,* Sept., 1932, p. 11.
13*Ibid.,* Dec., 1932, p. 9.
14*H. C. Journal,* Mar., 1933, p. 15.
15*Ibid., May,* 1938.
16Miller, O. O., "The Mennonite Board of Education and Her Schools," *Gospel Herald,* May 20, 1937, pp. 171-172.
17*H. C. Catalogs.*
18Local board notes.

[19]*H. C. Catalog*, 1935-36.
[20]Minutes of administrative cabinet, Jan. 30, 1938.
[21]*H. C. Journal*, Aug.-Sept., 1936.
[22]Minutes of administrative cabinet, May 2, 1938.
[23]*H. C. Journal*, Jan., 1938.
[24]Local board notes, June 11, 1937.
[25]*H. C. Journal*, Aug.-Sept., 1936.
[26]*Ibid.*
[27]*H. C. Catalog*, 1936-37.
[28]Meeting of Mennonite Board of Education, Feb. 18-19, 1935, *Gospel Herald*, Apr. 18, 1935, p. 61.
[29]"Statement of Policies of the Mennonite Board of Education," *Ibid.*, May 16, 1935, p. 156.
[30]Faculty meeting notes, Oct. 31, 1933.
[31]*Ibid.*, May 21, 1935.
[32]Official school notes, 1934-35.
[33]*Ibid.*, 1935-36.
[34]Smith, J. H., "First Impressions," *Ibid.*, Sept., 1934, p. 72.
[35]Henard, Leonard, "Boost Your School," *H. C. Journal*, Oct., 1937, p. 3.
[36]"Meeting of Mennonite Board of Education," *Gospel Herald*, Feb. 19-20, 1940, pp. 1037-38.
[37]Local board notes, Sept. 16, 1938; Jan. 21, 1938.
[38]*H. C. Journal*, Mar., 1940.
[39]Stoltzfus, Edna Fern, *H. C. Journal*, May, 1941, p. 8, Oct. 30, 1945.
[40]*Ibid.*, Miller, Wilma.
[41]Minutes of administrative cabinet, Sept. 24, 1940.
[42]Local board notes, Jan. 25, 1941.
[43]*H. C. Journal*, Jan., 1942.
[44]Miller, O. O., "Freeing Our Colleges of Debt," *Gospel Herald*, Sept. 17, 1942, p. 544.
[45]*Ibid.*, Feb. 11, 1943, p. 992.
[46]Minutes of Executive Committee of the Board of Education, Nov. 2, 1942.
[47]Faculty meeting notes, Dec. 23, 1943.
[48]Official school notes, 1942-43.
[49]*H.C. Catalog*, 1943-44, p. 31.
[50]"Plan of Study for the Th.B. Degree," *Gospel Herald*, Mar. 5, 1942, pp. 1045-1046.
[51]*H. C. Catalog*, 1941-42, p. 31.
[52]*H. C. Journal*, Sept., 1940.
[53]*H. C. Journal*, May, 1941, p. 11.
[54]Local board notes, Sept. 15, 1939.
[55]*Lark*, 1941.
[56]*Gospel Herald*, Oct. 26, 1939, p. 651-3.
[57]*H. C. Journal*, Jan., 1942, p. 16.
[58]*Ibid.*, Jan., 1942, p. 16.
[59]Minutes of administrative committee, Apr. 21, 1942.
[60]*Gospel Herald*, July 2, 1942, pp. 228-9.
[61]Faculty meeting notes, May 22, 1944.
[62]*Gospel Herald*, Oct. 28, 1943, p. 648.
[63]*Ibid.*, Apr. 28, 1944, pp. 77-78.
[64]*H. C. Journal*, Jan. 15, 1946, p. 1.
[65]*Ibid.*, Mar. 8, 1946.
[66]*Ibid.*, Feb. 28, 1946.
[67]*Ibid.*, Mar. 8, 1946.
[68]*Ibid.*, Mar. 29, 1946, p. 1
[69]Minutes of administrative committee, Feb. 26, 1946.

[70]*Ibid.*
[71]Minutes of Executive Committee of Board of Education, Aug. 24, 1946.
[72]*H. C. Journal,* Nov. 8, 1947.
[73]Annual Report of Hesston College for 1947-48.
[74]*Ibid.*
[75]Faculty meeting notes, 1948.
[76]*H. C. Journal,* Feb. 15, 1949.
[77]Official school notes, 1948-49.
[78]*Ibid.,* Nov. 19, 1949.
[79]*Ibid.,* Nov. 11, 1950.
[80]Minutes of Executive Committee of Mennonite Board of Education, May 11, 1951.
[81]*Ibid.,* May 20-21, 1950.
[82]*H. C. Journal,* June 30, 1945-46.
[83]Faculty meeting notes, Feb. 5, 1945-46.
[84]*Ibid.,* May 14, 1946.
[85]*Ibid.,* Nov. 9, 1949-50.
[86]*Ibid.,* May 14, 1946.
[87]Faculty meeting notes, Apr. 2, 1947.
[88]*Ibid.,* May 19, 1947.
[89]Notes of College Executive Committee, Apr. 26, 1945-46.
[90]*Ibid.,* Dec. 13, 1948.
[91]Faculty meeting notes, Oct. 10, 1944.
[92]*Ibid.,* Dec. 5, 1945.
[93]*Ibid.,* Nov. 13, 1945.
[94]Published Report of the Faculty Study Committee.
[95]*H. C. Journal,* Mar. 6, 1948, p. 1.
[96]Faculty meeting notes, Dec. 19, 1949.
[97]*Ibid.,* May 3, 1950.
[98]*Ibid.,* Sept. 17, 1947-48.
[99]Minutes of Board of Education, Feb. 16, 17, 1948.
[100]"Board of Education Notes," *Gospel Herald,* Oct. 4, 1949, p. 978.
[101]*H. C. Journal,* Feb. 21, 1948, p. 1.
[102]Administrative council notes, 1950-51.
[103]Minutes of administrative cabinet, Apr. 28, 1947.
[104]Dean's Annual Report, 1947-48.
[105]Faculty meeting notes, Oct. 17, 1945.
[106]Minutes of Executive Committee of Mennonite Board of Education, Sept. 17, 18, 1948.
[107]*H. C. Journal,* Mar. 14, 1949.
[108]*Ibid.,* Mar. 8, 1946, p. 956.
[109]Minutes of Executive Committee of the Board of Education, May 26, 1950.
[110]Minutes of Board of Education, Oct. 20-21, 1950.
[111]*H. C. Journal,* June 28, 1951, p. 1.
[112]*Ibid.*

CHAPTER VI

[1]Minutes of Executive Committee of Board of Education, May 26, 1950.
[2]*Ibid.,* Oct. 19-21, 1950.
[3]*Ibid.,* "Kauffman Explains Administrative Plan," Oct. 1, 1951.
[4]*H. C. Catalog,* 1951-52.
[5]Minutes of faculty meetings, Sept. 19, 1951.
[6]Minutes of Administrative Council, Oct. 24, 1951.

[7]Minutes of faculty meetings, Oct. 26, 1951.
[8]*Ibid.,* Oct. 31, 1951.
[9]*Ibid.,* Nov. 7, 1951.
[10]*Ibid.,* Nov. 28, 1951.
[11]*H. C. Journal,* Mar. 10, 1952.
[12]*Ibid.,* April 7, 1952.
[13]*Ibid.,* April 7, 1952.
[14]*Ibid.,* Mar. 18, 1953.
[15]Dean's Annual Report of Hesston College and Bible School for Year 1952-53.
[16]Minutes of faculty meetings, Dec. 10, 1952.
[17]Annual Report of Hesston College and Bible School for the Year 1952-53.
[18]"The Price of a Good Education," *H. C. Journal,* Dec. 12, 1945.
[19]*Ibid.,* Sept. 24, 1952.
[20]*Ibid.,* Nov. 25, 1950.
[21]*This Month,* June, 1953.
[22]Copy of president's speech.
[23]*H. C. Catalog,* 1953-55.
[24]Holsinger, Justus, *Faculty Study Project of the Hesston College and Bible School Curriculum,* p. 90.
[25]Minutes of faculty meetings, Sept. 16, 1953.
[26]*Ibid.,* Sept. 30, 1953.
[27]President's Memo, Aug. 26, 1945.
[28]President's Memo, Oct. 19, 1954.
[29]*This Month,* Oct., 1955.
[30]Report of President of Hesston College and Bible School to the South Central Conference, Aug. 22, 1956.
[31]*H.C.B.S. Bulletin,* Annual Report of President for Year 1953-54.
[32]President's Memo, April 19, 1955.
[33]*H. C. Journal,* Sept. 24, 1954.
[34]*This Month,* Nov., 1955.
[35]*H. C. Journal,* April 11, 1956.
[36]*Ibid.,* April 22, 1956.
[37]*This Month,* Jan., 1957.
[38]*H. C. Journal,* Nov. 5, 1956.
[39]Minutes of Administrative Committee, April 29, 1952.
[40]*This Month,* June, 1953.
[41]*Ibid.,* Aug., 1953.
[42]*H. C. Journal,* Feb. 4, 1955.
[43]*This Month,* Jan., 1956.
[44]*Ibid.,* Jan., 1956.
[45]Program of Dedication.
[46]*Gospel Herald,* June 5, 1956.
[47]*H. C. Bulletin,* Annual Report for Year 1952-53.
[48]Minutes of Executive Committee of Mennonite Board of Education, Oct. 15, 1954.
[49]*H. C. Journal,* May 22, 1956.
[50]*Ibid.,* May 12, 1954.
[51]President's Memo, Jan. 31, 1958.
[52]Faculty Meeting Notes, Mar. 4, 1953.
[53]Budget Work Sheet, 1953-54.
[54]Adm. Committee Minutes, Dec. 12, 1951.
[55]*This Month,* Oct., 1954.
[56]*Ibid.,* Aug., 1954.
[57]*Ibid.,* May, 1956.
[58]President's Memo, May 24, 1955.
[59]*This Month,* Jan., 1956.

[60]*Ibid.*, May, 1956.
[61]*H. C. Journal,* Sept. 10, 1957.
[62]*H. C. Catalogs.*
[63]*H. C. Bulletin,* Dec., 1957.
[84]*This Month,* April, 1953.
[65]*H. C. Journal,* Jan. 28, 1957.
[66]*Ibid.,* Oct. 8, 1952.
[67]*This Month,* June, 1956.
[68]*H. C. Journal,* Mar. 4, 1952.

CHAPTER VII

[1]*H. C. Journal,* Nov. 23, 1954.

APPENDICES

APPENDIX I

EDUCATIONAL PHILOSOPHY AND OBJECTIVES OF HESSTON COLLEGE AND BIBLE SCHOOL

Education promotes the greatest development of each individual along with the ability to participate and share in his society. The greatest development of the individual concerns itself with the whole of life—spiritual, intellectual, social, and physical. Education is not merely an accumulation of facts, but is also an awakening. It is a continuous process, and normally continues throughout life.

Education involves at least five essential factors: the learner, the teacher, the curriculum, the equipment, and the environment. The greatest of these is the learner. We believe that each student is different from every other student in interests, abilities, and needs. We believe that each student must be treated as an individual. It is the school's responsibility to know each student in terms of his interests, needs, and abilities, and to lead each one to his own discovery of the same, giving opportunity to pursue that ability to its maximum development. Every student has within him the ability to learn. It is the school's responsibility to stimulate the desire to learn. One great contribution of education is to develop within the learner an inquiring mind, the ability to withhold judgment, the power to think independently, and the ability to interpret creatively.

The teacher is the second major factor in education. Each member of the staff must be adequately prepared in the field in which he teaches, but in addition to this, he must have a broad cultural education which will aid him in seeing the whole of the process and not just in terms of his particular field or division. He should be continually growing in knowledge. As soon as the teacher ceases to learn, he ceases to teach. He should lead rather than drive students to the threshold of truth. He should teach because he loves teaching. We believe that each member of the staff should be chosen by the head of the school with the approval of the faculty and the Board of Education. The staff should be sufficient in number to enable each teacher to have time to plan his work without frustration. Finally, we believe that the teachers of Hesston College should be Christians of blameless integrity, loyal to the Mennonite Church, with strong courage, ingenious resources, and strong belief in their profession. Through qualities of foresight, patience, unselfishness, fairness, and sympathetic understanding, they should be able to guide students.

The above statements in regard to the learner and the teacher of Hesston College will require a curriculum which is adequate in its offerings—flexible and adaptable to each learner's needs. Each student will plan his curriculum in cooperation with the faculty. It will contribute to his "whole" development. There will be a variety of religious, vocational, cultural, social, and physical activities; because learning is a result of activity and cannot occur without activity.

There will be opportunities to discover vocational fields and to prepare toward a definite vocation. The organization and government of the curricular activities—classroom and the so-called extracurricular activities—will be cooperative, exercising freedom with control. Every learning activity will be purposeful. The curriculum of Hesston College will provide ample opportunity for the development of right attitudes toward God, self, family, friends, community, church, and state. Subject matter is of concern only to the extent that it aids in the kind of development stated above.

The fourth factor of education is the equipment or school plant. The equipment shall provide for the kind of education Hesston College proposes to offer. The library, central and classroom, is of major importance. The kind and number of books, periodicals, etc., will depend upon the number of students and upon the curriculum. At no time will the library arrive at the place of perfection, but it should be continually growing, meeting the needs of each year's students and each year's curriculum. The housing, recreational, and all instructional equipment needs should be adequately met.

The last factor involved in education is the environment which includes the school's relation to state and society. We believe the school should be a servant of the church, community, and state. It should lead the way to living the Christ Life. The school should be ready to share its resources with the community and constituency, consistent with its philosophy and objectives. The school should meet the Church and State requirements, keeping in touch with the state department of education as well as the Mennonite Board of Education. It should be above reproach in every respect.

In Conclusion:

We believe that students can be happy in school; that education must be thought of in terms of growth; that learning comes by doing; that life does not begin when school ends; but school is life. We believe that a knowledge of what the Bible teaches regarding the way of life should be the standard set by all who enter and leave the halls of our institution.

APPENDIX II

RELIGIOUS PHILOSOPHY OF HESSTON COLLEGE
AND BIBLE SCHOOL

Hesston College and Bible School accepts the Bible as the Word of God. This Word is the final authority. Man is depraved. The sacrifice of Christ for the sins of man is efficacious. Those who reject the atonement of Christ are eternally lost. Man realizes the highest good when he accepts Jesus Christ, the Son of God, as his personal Saviour, and as Lord of every detail in his life. This way of life is accepted by faith, and will express itself in one's conduct, will result in discipleship, and will obligate the believer to propagate the Gospel.

We believe that the tenets of the Mennonite Church are scriptural, that the Mennonite Church has a message for the world in which we live, and that Christian education is a part of the greater witness and mission of the church.

The religious objectives of Hesston College and Bible School are to fit her students to live in perfect harmony with the will of God by:

I. Leading all students to a vital faith in Christ.

II. Teaching students to know, appreciate, and use the Word of God.

III. Developing distinctively Christian personalities.

IV. Upholding a rigorous ethical ideal.

V. Kindling a vision of the world's need, and of the Christian's mission to meet that need.

VI. Giving actual training for Christian service, both by instruction and by the provision of opportunities for activity.

VII. Giving thorough indoctrination in matters of Christian faith.

VIII. Equipping students to fit into the life and work of their home congregations and of the church at large.

APPENDIX III
ENROLLMENT DATA

Year	High School	College	Normal for Elementary Teachers	Special Bible Term	Totals
1909-10	67			16	
1910-11	76			14	
1911-12	99			15	
1912-13	122			17	
1913-14	106			15	
1914-15	107			20	
1915-16	108	8		33	
1916-17	102	14		24	
1917-18	88	11		51	
1918-19	115	14		57	187
1919-20	152	20		60	239
1920-21	172	29		42	242
1921-22	184	26		19	230
1922-23	166	33		23	217
1923-24	142	37		19	194
1924-25	146	33		15	190
1925-26	158	45		24	227
1926-27	165	49		31	246
1927-28	193	56		24	273
1928-29	167	72		15	254
1929-30	118	61	8	19	206
1930-31	106	39	8	18	171
1931-32	64	20		16	100
1932-33	76			56	132
1933-34	109	37		71	217
1934-35	100	41		73	214
1935-36	123	45		85	253
1936-37	155	39		94	288
1937-38	145	59		99	303
1938-39	128	72	8	82	290
1939-40	139	71	19	74	303
1940-41	125	85	16	73	299
1941-42	139	77		71	287
1942-43	180	66		51	297
1943-44	235	48		36	319
1944-45	255	38		33	325
1945-46					
1946-47	247	93		47	396 (incl. 9 Chr. Workers, 10 Th.B.)
1947-48	181	116	17	78	392
1948-49	182	133	32	59	406
1949-50	211	114	37	44	406
1950-51	202	136	24	56	418
1951-52	222	127	9	47	405
1952-53	223	189		34	446
1953-54	196	173		31	400
1954-55	175	132		53	360
1955-56	191	121		7	319
1956-57	176	140			316
1957-58	161	181			342
1958-59	168	181			349

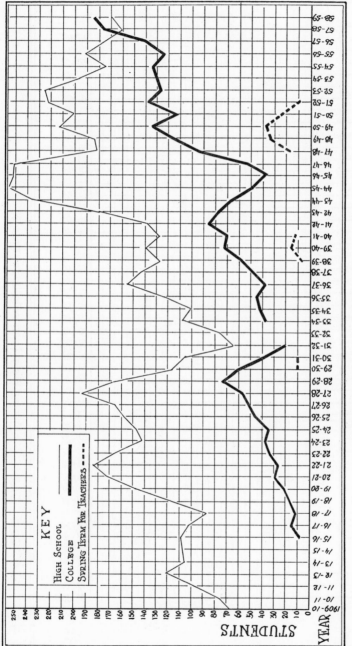

Enrollment graph for the fifty-year period.

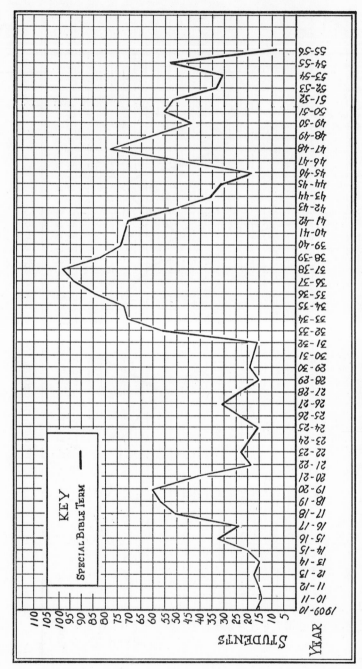

Winter Bible Term enrollment graph.

APPENDIX IV

PRESIDENTS AND DEANS

Presidents

D. H. Bender..............................1909-1930
Milo Kauffman..............................1932-1951
Roy D. Roth, President-elect......1951-1953
        President................1953-1959

Deans

J. D. Charles...............................1919-1923
Noah Oyer...................................1923-1924
Edward Yoder..............................1924-1928 on leave of absence
                      1928-1932
Paul Erb......................................1924-1928 acting dean
                      1932-1941 dean
Ivan R. Lind...............................1941-1949
Walter E. Oswald.......................1949-1953
Just is G. Holsinger..................1953-1959

APPENDIX V

ADMINISTRATIVE COMMITTEES

Year President Principal	Dean	Registrar	Business Manager	Dean of Student Personnel	Director of Public Relations	Extra Member
1909-10—D. H. Bender		J. D. Charles	T. M. Erb			
1910-11—D. H. Bender		J. D. Charles	T. M. Erb			
1911-12—D. H. Bender		J. D. Charles	T. M. Erb			
1912-13—D. H. Bender		J. D. Charles	T. M. Erb			
1913-14—D. H. Bender		J. D. Charles	T. M. Erb			
1914-15—D. H. Bender		J. D. Charles	T. M. Erb			
1915-16—D. H. Bender		J. D. Charles	T. M. Erb			
1916-17—D. H. Bender		J. D. Charles	T. M. Erb			
1917-18—D. H. Bender		J. D. Charles	T. M. Erb			
1918-19—D. H. Bender		J. D. Charles	T. M. Erb			
1919-20—D. H. Bender	J. D. Charles	J. D. Charles	T. M. Erb			
1920-21—D. H. Bender	J. D. Charles	J. D. Charles	T. M. Erb			
1921-22—D. H. Bender	J. D. Charles	J. D. Charles	T. M. Erb			
1922-23—D. H. Bender	J. D. Charles	J. D. Charles	T. M. Erb			
1923-24—D. H. Bender	Noah Oyer	Noah Oyer	T. M. Erb			
1924-25—D. H. Bender	Paul Erb (acting)	S. E. Miller	T. M. Erb			
1925-26—D. H. Bender	Paul Erb (acting)	S. E. Miller	T. M. Erb			
1926-27—D. H. Bender	Paul Erb (acting)	S. E. Miller	T. M. Erb			
1927-28—D. H. Bender	Paul Erb (acting)	S. E. Miller	T. M. Erb			
1928-29—D. H. Bender	Edward Yoder	S. E. Miller	S. E. Miller (ass't)			
1929-30—D. H. Bender	Edward Yoder	Paul Erb	S. E. Miller			(Bible Dept.)
1930-31	Edward Yoder	Paul Erb	M. A. Yoder			Irvin Burkhart
1931-32	Edward Yoder	Paul Erb	M. A. Yoder			Irvin Burkhart
1932-33—Milo Kauffman	Paul Erb	Paul Erb	(1)			
1933-34—Milo Kauffman	Paul Erb	Paul Erb	(1)			
1934-35—Milo Kauffman	Paul Erb	D. D. Driver	(2)			
1935-36—Milo Kauffman	Paul Erb	D. D. Driver	(2)			
1936-37—Milo Kauffman	Paul Erb	D. D. Driver	(2)			
1937-38—Milo Kauffman	Paul Erb	D. D. Driver	(2)			

238

Year	President Principal	Dean	Registrar	Business Manager	Dean of Student Personnel	Director of Public Relations	Extra Member
1938-39	Milo Kauffman	Paul Erb	D. D. Driver	(2)			
1939-40	Milo Kauffman	Paul Erb	D. D. Driver	(3)			
1940-41	Milo Kauffman	Paul Erb-Ivan R. Lind	D. D. Driver	(3)			
1941-42	Milo Kauffman	Ivan R. Lind	D. D. Driver	(3)	J. H. Koppenhaver		
1942-43	Milo Kauffman	Ivan R. Lind	D. D. Driver	(3)	J. H. Koppenhaver		
1943-44	Milo Kauffman	Ivan R. Lind	D. D. Driver		J. H. Koppenhaver		
1944-45	Milo Kauffman	Ivan R. Lind	D. D. Driver		J. H. Koppenhaver		
1945-46	Milo Kauffman	Ivan R. Lind	D. D. Driver	Paul Wittrig	J. H. Koppenhaver		
1946-47	Milo Kauffman	Ivan R. Lind	Ivan R. Lind	Daniel E. Kauffman	J. H. Koppenhaver		
1947-48	Milo Kauffman	Ivan R. Lind		Daniel E. Kauffman	J. H. Koppenhaver		
1948-49	Milo Kauffman	Ivan R. Lind	(4)	Daniel E. Kauffman	Walter E. Oswald		
1949-50	Milo Kauffman	Walter E. Oswald	(4)	Daniel E. Kauffman	Walter E. Oswald		
1950-51	Milo Kauffman	Walter E. Oswald	(4)	Daniel E. Kauffman	Walter E. Oswald / Leonard L. Lichti (1 Sem. each)		
1951-52	Roy D. Roth (Elect)	Walter E. Oswald	(4)	Daniel E. Kauffman	Leonard L. Lichti	Merle L. Bender (Lv. of Absence)	
1952-53	Roy D. Roth (Elect)	Walter E. Oswald	Justus G. Holsinger	Daniel E. Kauffman	Leonard L. Lichti	Merle L. Bender (Lv. of Absence)	
1953-54	Roy D. Roth	Justus G. Holsinger		Daniel E. Kauffman	Leonard L. Lichti	Merle L. Bender	
1954-55	Roy D. Roth	Justus G. Holsinger		Daniel E. Kauffman	Leonard L. Lichti	Merle L. Bender	
1955-56	Roy D. Roth	Justus G. Holsinger		Daniel E. Kauffman	Leonard L. Lichti	Merle L. Bender	
1956-57	Roy D. Roth	Justus G. Holsinger	Leonard L. Lichti	Kenneth E. King (acting)		Merle L. Bender	
1957-58	Roy D. Roth	Justus G. Holsinger	(5)	Daniel E. Kauffman			Mary Miller / Paul A. Friesen
1958-59	Roy D. Roth	Justus G. Holsinger		Daniel E. Kauffman			Paul Bender / John P. Duerksen

(1) A. N. Troyer—acting Business Manager 1932-34, but was not a part of the committee.
(2) Amos Gingerich—Business Manager 1934-1939, but was not a part of the committee.
(3) L. L. Swartzendruber—Business Manager 1939-43, but was not a part of the committee.
(4) Gladys Winn—Acting Registrar 1948-52, but was not a part of the committee.
(5) Leonard L. Lichti—Registrar 1957-58, but was not a part of the committee.

239

APPENDIX VI

FACULTY

D. H. Bender............................1909-1930
J. D. Charles............................1909-1923
J. B. Kanagy............................1909-1910, 1913-1918
Stella Cooprider............................1909-1912 (part time)
T. M. Erb............................1909-1929 (Business Manager)
Esther Lehman............................1910-1913
W. W. Oesch............................1910-1912
Noah L. Good............................1910-1911 (part time)
Martha Shenk............................1910-1911 (part time)
J. B. Smith............................1911-1917, 1928-1932
M. D. Landis............................1911-1928
George M. Hostetler............................1911-1912 (part time)
Alta Mae Eby Erb............................1912-1918, 1919-1943
Grace Cooprider............................1912-1914 (part time)
Mary Gish............................1913-1914
Siddie King............................1913-1919 (part time)
Paul Erb............................1913-1916 (part time) 1919-1941
J. A. Ressler............................1913-1914 (part time)
Mary Ramer............................1914-1915
Marian Charlton............................1915-1917
Chester K. Lehman............................1916-1919
Viola Wenger............................1916-1919 (part time)
Noah Oyer............................1917-1921, 1922-1924
Edward Yoder............................1917-1921 (part time) 1928-1933
Edward Diener............................1917-1918 (part time)
Harold S. Bender............................1918-1921
D. D. Driver............................1918-1919, 1922-1923 (part time) 1923-
Margaret Horst............................1918-1921, 1924-25 (part time) 1925-31
Chris Graber............................1918-1919, 1920-1921 (part time)
Keturah Kauffman............................1918-1919 (part time)
Arthur Slagell............................1919-1920
Mary Mensch............................1919-1920
Esther Good............................1919-1924 (part time) 1924-1932
Paul Bender............................1919-1921 (part time) 1921-23, 1925-28,
⠀⠀⠀⠀⠀⠀⠀⠀⠀⠀⠀⠀⠀⠀⠀⠀⠀⠀⠀⠀⠀⠀⠀⠀⠀⠀⠀⠀⠀⠀⠀⠀1929-33, 1958-
S. M. Kanagy............................1920-1924
Gustav Enss............................1920-1927
Silas Hertzler............................1920-1921
S. Enos Miller............................1920-1932
Kathryn Miller............................1920-1923 (part time) 1923-1924
Bertha Burkholder............................1920-1922, 1923-1924 (part time)
Albert Classen............................1921-1922
M. T. Brackbill............................1921-1923 (part time)
Paul Synder............................1921-1922 (part time)
Salina Jennings............................1922-1923 (part time)
Peter Friesen............................1923-1924 (part time)
Guy Hershberger............................1923-1924
Joseph D. Graber............................1923-1924 (part time)
S. M. King............................1924-1930
Abraham Albrecht............................1924-1927

Glenn Hershberger	1924-1925
Alvin Yordy	1924-1926 (part time) 1927-1928
Bertha Berkey	1924-1928 (part time)
Milo Kauffman	1924-1925 (part time) 1926-1928, 1931-1951
	1951- (part time)
Elmer Flaming	1924-1925 (part time)
Irvin Burkhart	1924-1925 (part time) 1929-1933
Mary Miller	1924-1926 (part time) 1926-1932, 1937-1945, 1947-
Andrew Glick	1925-1927 (part time) 1927-1932
Ruth Bender	1925-1927 (part time) 1927-1930
John Hershberger	1925-1927 (part time)
Fred Brenneman	1925-1927 (part time)
J. N. Byler	1926-1942
Mrs. Gustav Enss	1926-1928 (part time)
Maurice A. Yoder	1927-1932, 1934-
Charles Fricke	1928-1932
J. B. Epp	1928-1931
Verna Enns	1928-1930 (part time) 1930-1931, 1937-40
Phoebe Yoder	1928-1930 (part time)
Mrs. Maurice A. Yoder	1929-1931, 1934-1943 (part time)
Jesse Hartzler	1929-1932 (part time)
Cornelius Wall	1930-1932
Alta Housour	1932-1940
J. N. Weaver	1934-1940
J. Harold Smith	1934-1944
Samuel Swartz	1935-1937
Bertha Nitzsche	1938-1950
Ivan R. Lind	1938-1950, 1952-1958
J. P. Duerksen	1939-1944, 1948-1955, 1958-
J. H. Koppenhaver	1939-1947
Wilmer Landis	1941-1944
Eli Stoltzfus	1941-1944
Ethel Climenhaga	1943-1948
Edwin I. Weaver	1944-1948, 1957-
Eva Yeackley	1944-1945
Melva Kauffman	1944-
Lois Litwiller	1944-1947
Marian Messner	1944-1951
Verna Burkholder	1944-1947
Esther Weber	1945-1955
Trusie Zook	1945-1947
Glenn L. Hershberger	1945-1949
Walter E. Oswald	1945-1954
Alice Buckwalter	1945-1950
Arnold Dietzel	1945-1946, 1954-1955
Daniel E. Kauffman	1946-
E. Freedley Schrock	1946-
Mrs. Fred Yoder	1946-1948
Naomi Brubaker	1946-1950
Laurence Horst	1946-1952
Milton Vogt	1946-1948
Orpha Zimmerly	1946-1955
John Steiner	1947-1950
Paul E. Yoder	1947-1949
Cleda Holdeman	1947-1950

A PILLAR OF CLOUD

Christine Blosser............................1947-1950
Gladys Winn................................1948-1952
Gideon G. Yoder............................1948-
Clayton Beyler.............................1949-
Ellen M. Miller...........................1949-
Vincent J. Krabill........................1949-
Willard Conrad............................1949-1956
Ruth Harder...............................1949-1952
Kenneth E. King...........................1949-
B. F. Hartzler............................1949-51 (part time) 1954-1955 (part time)
Lester Culp...............................1950-1955
Beulah Litwiller..........................1950-1951
Wanda Tieszen.............................1950-1954 (part time)
Harold Yoder..............................1950-1951
Roy D. Roth...............................1951-1959
Leonard L. Lichti.........................1951-
Evelyn I. Rouner..........................1951-1956
Vernon Allison............................1951-1952
Lowell J. Byler...........................1951-1953, 1955-1958
Miriam K. Byler...........................1951-1953, 1955-1958
Evan Oswald...............................1951-
Merle L. Bender...........................1951-1957
Lena Waltner..............................1952-1953 (part time)
Orval Shoemaker...........................1952-1954
Justus G. Holsinger.......................1952-
John Landis...............................1952-1953
Dorothea M. Eigsti........................1952-
Mary Eleanor Bender.......................1953-1955
Gail Miller...............................1953-1958
Paul Marvin Yoder.........................1953-1958
Calvin W. Redekop.........................1954-1956, 1959-
Carolyn B. Roth...........................1954-1955 (part time)
Alice B. Reschly..........................1954-
Clifford W. Amstutz.......................1954-
Joan Good.................................1954-1958
Alice T. Miller...........................1955-1957
Kenneth W. Steider........................1955-
Wandalee Weaver...........................1955-1957
J. Winfield Fretz.........................1955-1958 (part time)
John Rogalsky.............................1955-1956 (part time)
Eugene A. Miller..........................1955-1957
Ray Kauffman..............................1955-1956
Wilma Toews...............................1955-1956
Paul A. Friesen...........................1956-
Reynold Sawatzky..........................1956-
Peter Dyck................................1956-1957 (part time)
Mrs. Esko Loewen..........................1957-1958 (part time)
Mrs. Edwin I. Weaver......................1957-
Mae Nitzsche..............................1957-1959
Harold Miller.............................1957-1958
Jacob Nickel..............................1957-1958 (part time)
Sara Ann Claassen.........................1958-
Janeth Nichols............................1958-
Marvin Miller.............................1958-
Mrs. Eva Harshbarger......................1958-1959 (part time)
Mrs. Fay Zook.............................1958- (part time)
Myrtle Hamilton...........................1959-

242

APPENDIX VII
LIBRARIANS

Librarian	Assistant to Librarian
1909-10—J. D. Charles	
1910-11—W. W. Oesch	Roy Ebersole
1911-12—Esther Lehman	
1912-13—Esther Lehman	Lucy Yoder
1913-14—Alta Mae Eby	Rose Shank
1914-15—Alta Mae Eby	Rose Shank
1915-16—Alta Mae Eby	Rose Shank
1916-17—Alta Mae Eby	Rose Shank
1917-18—Alta Mae Erb	Rose Shank
1918-19—Alta Mae Erb	Margaret Horst
1919-20—Alta Mae Erb	Margaret Horst
1920-21—Alta Mae Erb	Margaret Horst
1921-22—Alta Mae Erb	Margaret Horst
1922-23—Alta Mae Erb	Margaret Horst
1923-24—Alta Mae Erb	Margaret Horst
1924-25—Alta Mae Erb	Nellie Zook
1925-26—Alta Mae Erb	Nellie Zook
1926-27—Alta Mae Erb	Andrew Glick
1927-28—Alta Mae Erb	Andrew Glick
1928-29—Andrew Glick	Joseph Weaver
	Harold Sommerfeld
1929-30—Andrew Glick	Harold Sommerfeld
	Clifford Stutzman
1930-31—Paul Erb	Bertha Nitzsche
1931-32—Paul Erb	Bertha Nitzsche
1932-33—Paul Erb	Bertha Nitzsche
1933-34—Paul Erb	Bertha Nitzsche
1934-35—Paul Erb	Jesse Roth
1935-36—Paul Erb	
1936-37—Bertha Nitzsche	
1937-38—Bertha Nitzsche	
1938-39—Bertha Nitzsche	
1939-40—Bertha Nitzsche	
1940-41—Bertha Nitzsche	
1941-42—Bertha Nitzsche	
1942-43—Bertha Nitzsche	
1943-44—Bertha Nitzsche	
1944-45—Bertha Nitzsche	
1945-46—Esther Weber	
1946-47—Esther Weber	
1947-48—Esther Weber	
—Alice Buckwalter, Acting Librarian, (1st semester)	
1948-49—Esther Weber	Alice Buckwalter
1949-50—Esther Weber	
1950-51—Esther Weber	
1951-52—Esther Weber	Mrs. Leo Miller
1952-53—Esther Weber	Mrs. Kenneth E. King
1953-54—Esther Weber	Mrs. Kenneth E. King
1954-55—Esther Weber	Mrs. Kenneth E. King
1955-56—Kenneth W. Steider	Mrs. Kenneth E. King
1956-57—Kenneth W. Steider	Mrs. Kenneth E. King
1957-58—Kenneth W. Steider	Mrs. Kenneth E. King
1958-59—Kenneth W. Steider	Mrs. Kenneth E. King

APPENDIX VIII
PERSONNEL OFFICIALS

Year	Dean of Personnel	Dean of Men	Dean of Women	Matrons	Assistant Matrons	Hall Manager	Assistant Hall Managers
1909-10				Stella Cooprider		J. B. Kanagy	John Hilty
1910-11				Stella Cooprider Esther Lehman		J. B. Kanagy	John Hilty
1911-12				Stella Cooprider Esther Lehman		Steve Yoder	
1912-13				Grace Cooprider (3 terms) Hannah Brenneman (1 term)		Steve Yoder	
1913-14				Mary Gish (1 term) Alta Mae Eby (3 terms)		David Miller (2 terms) Noah Oyer (2 terms)	
1914-15				Siddie King Alta Mae Eby	Marian Charlton	Noah Oyer	Philip Mack
1915-16				Siddie King Alta Mae Eby	Marian Charlton	Noah Oyer	Philip Mack
1916-17				Siddie King Alta Mae Eby		Noah Oyer	Ray Bender
1917-18				Siddie King Alta Mae Eby		Noah Oyer	Edward Yoder
1918-19				Siddie Oyer	Keturah Kauffman	Noah Oyer	Edward Yoder
1919-20				Siddie Oyer Mary Mensch	Mary Wenger	Edward Yoder	J. N. Byler
1920-21				Esther Good		Willard Smith	Titus Lapp
1921-22				Esther Good		S. M. Kanagy	I. E. Burkhart
1922-23			Mrs. Guy Hershberger	Mrs. S. M. Kanagy	Pearl Klopfenstein	S. M. Kanagy	I. E. Burkhart
1923-24			Margaret Horst	Mrs. S. M. Kanagy	Pearl Klopfenstein	Guy Hershberger	I. E. Burkhart
1924-25			Margaret Horst		Katie Yoder	I. E. Burkhart	Milo Kauffman
1925-26			Margaret Horst		Ida Hostetler	Milo Kauffman	Edward Roupp
1926-27			Esther Good		Ida Hostetler	Milo Kauffman	Edward Roupp
1927-28			Margaret Horst		Phoebe Yoder	Milo Kauffman	Paul Mininger
1928-29			Margaret Horst		Katie Reber	Paul Mininger	Nelson E. Kauffman
1929-30				Mrs. Maude Driver		Paul Mininger	Ezra Hershberger
1930-31				Margaret Horst	Salome Johnston	Ezra Hershberger	Paul Miller
1931-32			Mrs. I. E. Burkhart	Mrs. I. E. Burkhart	Fannie Schrock	Ezra Hershberger	Marcus Lind

Year	Dean of Personnel	Dean of Men	Dean of Women	Matrons	Assistant Matrons	Hall Manager	Assistant Hall Managers
1932-33			Alta Housour (acting)	Alta Housour		Vernon Roth	Jesse Roth
1933-34			Alta Housour	Alta Housour		Vernon Roth	
1934-35				Mrs. George Beare		George Beare	
1935-36			Mabel Hershberger (acting)	Mrs. Anna Holdeman	Gladys Weaver	Gideon G. Yoder	Walter Marner
1936-37		J. Harold Smith	Mary Miller	Pearl Kauffman	Lydia Driver	Walter Marner	Ivan Headings
1937-38		J. P. Duerksen (acting)	Mary Miller	Sara Nafziger	Mary White	Wilbert Nafziger	Ivan Headings
1938-39		J. Harold Smith		Fannie Schrock	Margaret Mininger	Ivan Headings	Leonard Henard
1939-40			Mary Miller	Ruth Duerksen	Alice Miller, Katie Yoder	John P. Duerksen	Edward Kenagy
1940-41—John H. Koppenhaver			Mary Miller	Ruth Duerksen	Alice Miller, Erma Zook	John P. Duerksen	Richard Showalter
1941-42—John H. Koppenhaver			Mary Miller	Katie Yoder	Edna Fern Stoltzfus	Paul Buckwalter	Samuel Janzen
1942-43—John H. Koppenhaver			Mary Miller	Katie Yoder	Alice Miller, Marie Duerksen, Genevieve Bishop	Marcus Bishop, Mervin Nafziger	
1943-44—John H. Koppenhaver			Mary Miller	Ethel Yoder	Beulah Shank, Rosalie Garber, Wilma Wenger, Ruby Gingerich	Edward Wiebe	Paul Friesen
1944-45—John H. Koppenhaver			Mary Miller	Katie Ropp, Beulah Stauffer	Erma Zook, Rosalie Garber, Rhoda Martin	Glenn L. Hershberger	Junior Flisher
1945-46—John H. Koppenhaver			Marian Messner	Katie Ropp, Trusie Zook	Rosalie Garber, Gladys Winn	Glenn L. Hershberger	
1946-47—John H. Koppenhaver			Marian Messner	Orpha Zimmerly, Mrs. Fred Yoder	Doris Burkey, Elsie Burkhart, Rosalie Garber	Laurence Horst	Frederick Erb
1947-48—Walter E. Oswald		Laurence Horst (acting)	Marian Messner	Orpha Zimmerly	Doris Burkey, Elsie Burkhart	Laurence Horst	Daniel Stoltzfus
1948-49—Walter E. Oswald		Laurence Horst	Marian Messner	Orpha Zimmerly	Marian Messner, Dorothy Gingerich, Carol Yoder, Dorothy Bender, Wilma Pletcher	LeRoy Bechler, Laurence Horst	James Snyder
1949-50—Walter E. Oswald		Laurence Horst	Orpha Zimmerly	Orpha Zimmerly	Carol Yoder, LaVerne Vogt, Irene Springer	John Mark Yoder, LeRoy Bechler	Roman Hershberger

Year	Dean of Personnel	Dean of Men	Dean of Women	Matrons	Assistant Matrons	Hall Manager	Assistant Hall Managers
1950-51	Walter E. Oswald (1st sem.) Leonard L. Lichti (2nd sem.)	Laurence Horst	Orpha Zimmerly	Orpha Zimmerly	Mildred Yoder Martha Duerksen Verlene Knepp	Chester Slagell James Detweiler	Nathan Nussbaum Wallace Jantz
1951-52	Leonard L. Lichti	Laurence Horst	Orpha Zimmerly	Orpha Zimmerly	Edith Shantz Martha Duerksen Martha King	Chester Slagell Elmer Miller	Evan Oswald John Zook
1952-53	Leonard L. Lichti	Orval Shoemaker	Orpha Zimmerly	Orpha Zimmerly	Martha Duerksen Sylvia Andres Dorothy Detweiler Dorthy Eigsti	Marvin Yoder	Merle Springer John Zook
1953-54	Leonard L. Lichti	Orval Shoemaker	Orpha Zimmerly	Orpha Zimmerly	Dorothy Detweiler Marie Schrock Rosella Kauffman Mrs. Dale Martin	James Kratz D. A. Raber	Wayne King Mark Conrad Dalton Hostetler Peter Hartman Dean Miller
1954-55		Paul Marvin Yoder	Orpha Zimmerly	Orpha Zimmerly Dorothy Detweiler	Rosa Beachy Laura Gerig	D. A. Raber Stanlee Kauffman Royce Roth Ira Zook, Jr.	
1955-56		Eugene A. Miller	Alice T. Miller	Dorothy Detweiler Mrs. Agness Detweiler	Erna Saltzman Noreen Cressman Margaret Litwiller	Ray Kauffman D. A. Raber Russell Shenk Harold Shetler	
1956-57		Eugene A. Miller	Alice T. Miller	Vera Kennel Erna Saltzman	Mary Brubacher Helen Lind Treva Swartzendruber Margaret Ann Steider	Leon Stutzman Curtis Dietz Marion Bontrager Paul Horst Howard Snyder Willard Ressler	
1957-58		Harold Miller	Mae Nitzsche	Mae Nitzsche Ruby Horst	Mary Brubacher Lavonne Gisel Mary Schantz Treva Swartzendruber Doris Waidelich	Laurel Miller Ronald Weaver Arnold Wyse Arnold Miller Howard Birky Ralph Kauffman	
1958-59		Leonard L. Lichti	Mae Nitzsche	Mae Nitzsche Mary Lee Heyerly	Mary Brubacher Twyla Selzer Lavonne Gisel Jeannene Reschly Betty Smith Carol Histand	Arnold Wyse Arnold Miller Aden Troyer Cecil Swartzendruber Samuel Strong John Blough Dwight Hershberger	

246

APPENDIX IX
STAFF

OFFICE ASSISTANTS, PHYSICIAN, AND NURSE

Year	Office Assistants	Physician	Nurse
1909-10			
1910-11	John Hilty		
1911-12	J. A. Cooprider		
	A. L. Hess		
1912-13			
1913-14	Grace Cooprider		
1914-15	Philip Mack		
1915-16			
1916-17			
1917-18			
1918-19			
1919-20	Susie Snyder		
1920-21	Susie Snyder		
	Leah Erb		
1921-22	Susie Snyder	Lavina Balmer	
	Leah Erb		
1922-23	Susie Snyder	Lavina Balmer	
	Leah Erb		
1923-24	Bertha Berkey		
	Susie Snyder		
	Esther Kulp		
	Margaret Horst		
1924-25	Bertha Berkey		
	Esther Kulp		
1925-26	Bertha Berkey		
	Esther Kulp		
1926-27	Bertha Berkey		Rhoda Yoder
	Esther Kulp		(short term)
			Lydia Heatwole
			(short term)
1927-28	Bertha Berkey		
	John Snyder (Bookkeeper)		
	Bertha Nitzsche		
1928-29	Bertha Nitzsche		
	John Snyder (Bookkeeper)		
	Verna Enns		
1929-30	John Snyder (Bookkeeper)		
	Bertha Nitzsche		
	Dessie Troyer		
1930-31	John Snyder (Bookkeeper)		
	Lois Winey		
	Bertha Nitzsche		
1931-32	John Snyder (Bookkeeper)		
	Lois Winey		
	Bertha Nitzsche		
1932-33	Lois Winey		
	Bertha Nitzsche		
1933-34	Bertha Nitzsche		
	Anna Hallman		
	Ruby Martin		

247

Year	Office Assistants	Physician	Nurse
1934-35	Bertha Nitzsche Anna Hallman		
1935-36	Bertha Nitzsche J. N. Weaver (Bookkeeper) Harry Wenger Louise Miller Rose Stauffer Wilma Smith		
1936-37	Bertha Nitzsche		
1937-38	Bertha Nitzsche (Bookkeeper) Verna Enns		Nora Miller
1938-39	Mrs. I. Mark Ross Bertha Nitzsche (Bookkeeper)		
1939-40	Bertha Nitzsche (Bookkeeper)		
1940-41	Bertha Nitzsche (Bookkeeper) Margaret Pursley		
1941-42	Arlene Sitler		Inez Snyder Barbara Lauber
1942-43	Bertha Nitzsche Helen Shetler Roberta Showalter Ethel Peaster Mary Ellen Miller Kathleen Erb Leta Miller Margaret Pursley	Fred S. Brenneman	
1943-44	Wilma Miller Opal Nitzsche Ruby Zook Gladys Zimmerman	Fred S. Brenneman	Margaret Risser
1944-45	Wilma Miller Rosalie Garber Roselena Willems Gladys Zimmerman Lois Stutzman	Fred S. Brenneman	Margaret Risser
1945-46	Rosalie Garber Ida Louise Sutter Donna Lou Byler	Fred S. Brenneman	Ophia Sevits Luella Gingerich
1946-47	Katie Ropp (Bookkeeper) Gladys Winn Ruby Zook Arletta Selzer	Fred S. Brenneman	Ophia Sevits Eeke van der Schaaf
1947-48	Katie Ropp (Accountant) Ruby Zook Laura Histand Leroy Kennel	Delbert Preheim	Lois Kanagy Ruth Cressman
1948-49	Mary Gerig Mrs. Merle Bender Laura Histand Katie Ropp (Accountant)	Fred S. Brenneman	Lois Kanagy Ruth Cressman
1949-50	Katie Ropp (Accountant) Laura Histand Florence Zehr	Fred S. Brenneman	Frances Lais

248

Year	Office Assistants	Physician	Nurse
1950-51	Katie Ropp (Accountant) Anne Hostetler Howard Bauman Faye Stalter Mrs. Roman Hershberger	Fred S. Brenneman Paul G. Brenneman	Frances Lais
1951-52	Katie Ropp (Accountant) Howard Bauman Mrs. Merle L. Bender Faye Stalter Esther Rediger Martha Duerksen	Fred S. Brenneman	Jeannette Lewis
1952-53	Katie Ropp (Accountant) Esther Rediger Wilma Hostetler Mrs. Alvin Kauffman Mildred Slagell	Fred S. Brenneman	Lois Kanagy
1953-54	Katie Ropp (Accountant) Esther Rediger Wilma Hostetler Mrs. Alvin Kauffman Mildred Slagell Mrs. Evan Oswald	Florence Friesen	Mrs. Walter Fenton
1954-55	Katie Ropp (Accountant) Mrs. Alvin Kauffman Wilma Hostetler Mildred Slagell Esther Rediger Sarah Anne Zook Carol Jean Roupp (summer)	Florence Friesen	Mamie Schrock
1955-56	Katie Ropp (Accountant) Wilma Hostetler Mildred Slagell Mrs. Calvin W. Redekop Sarah Anne Zook Kathryn Steckly	Fred S. Brenneman	Irene Bontrager
1956-57	Katie Ropp (Accountant) Mildred Slagell Mrs. Jess Kauffman Ruth Schweitzer Faye Birky Kathryn Steckly	Florence Friesen	Irene Hertzler
1957-58	Katie Ropp (Accountant) Mildred Slagell Lois Hershberger Kathryn Steckly Faye Birky Ruth Schweitzer	Wilmer Harms	Barbara Eberly
1958-59	Katie Ropp (Accountant) Carol Jean Roupp (Accountant) Mildred Slagell Joyce Hathaway Kathryn Steckly Mrs. James Horsch Ruth Schweitzer Carol Ratzloff	Wilmer Harms	Barbara Eberly

A PILLAR OF CLOUD

COOKS AND DIETITIAN

Year	Cooks	Dietitian
1909-10	Edna Beck Selzer	
	Mrs. J. A. Cooprider	
1910-11	Katie Swietzer	
1911-12	Susie Hostetler	
1912-13	Mr. and Mrs. J. P. Berkey	
1913-14	Fannie Miller	
1914-15	Fannie Miller	
1915-16	Fannie Miller	
	Myrtle Brunk	
1916-17		
1917-18	Myrtle Brunk	
1918-19	Myrtle Brunk	
1919-20	Lulu Kauffman	
	Gertie Troyer	
1920-21	Mrytle Brunk	
1921-22	Myrtle Brunk	
1922-23	Lydia Berkey	
1923-24	Mr. and Mrs. Ephraim Risser	
1924-25	Mr. and Mrs. Ephraim Risser	
1925-26	Mr. and Mrs. Ephraim Risser	
1926-27		
1927-28	Anna Horst	
	Florence Shirk	
1928-29	Mr. and Mrs. Ephraim Risser	
1929-30	Mr. and Mrs. Roy Troyer	
1930-31	Mr. and Mrs. Roy Troyer	
1931-32	Katie Saltzman	
1932-33	Katie Saltzman	
1933-34	Katie Saltzman	
1934-35	Mr. and Mrs. Glen Miller	
1935-36		
1936-37	Mr. and Mrs. Glen Miller	
1937-38	Mr. and Mrs. Glen Miller	
1938-39	Mrs. I. Mark Ross	
1939-40	Mrs. I. Mark Ross	
1940-41	Mrs. I. Mark Ross	
1941-42	Mrs. I. Mark Ross	Dora and Mabel Hostetler
1942-43	Elizabeth Shetler	
	Mary Schmidt	
1943-44	Hattie Sommerfeld	
	Edna King	
1944-45	Hattie Sommerfeld	
	Edna King	
1945-46	Katie Yoder	
1946-47	Archie Kauffman	Naomi Brubaker
	Harold Oswald	
	John Eichelberger	
	Elsie Selzer	
1947-48	Archie Kauffman	Naomi Brubaker
1948-49	Wayne Zimmerman	Naomi Brubaker
	Mrs. Ida Gerber	
	John Eichelberger	
1949-50	Wayne Zimmerman	Naomi Brubaker
	Mrs. Ida Gerber	
	John Eichelberger	

250

Year	Cooks	Dietitian
1950-51	Wayne Zimmerman Mrs. Ida Gerber Melvin Buller	Ruth Harder
1951-52	Wayne Zimmerman Mrs. Ida Gerber	Ruth Harder
1952-53	Wayne Zimmerman Emil Yoder Wayne Swartzendruber Effie Yoder	Ruth Harder
1953-54	Mrs. Ida Gerber Emil Yoder	Mrs. Menno Fast
1954-55	Emil Yoder Mrs. Ida Gerber Harold Troyer	Joan Good
1955-56	Emil Yoder Mrs. Ida Gerber Don Houser	Joan Good
1956-57	Emil Yoder Mrs. Ida Gerber	Joan Good
1957-58	Emil Yoder Paul Miller Mrs. Ida Gerber Clare Bechler	Joan Good
1958-59	Paul Miller Mrs. John Wenger Mrs. Ralph Myers, Jr. Mrs. Truman Miller	Janeth Nichols

SUPERINTENDENT OF BUILDINGS AND GROUNDS, SUPERINTENDENT OF FARM AND DAIRY, AND LAUNDRY SUPERVISOR

Year	Superintendent of Buildings & Grounds	Superintendent of Farm & Dairy	Laundry Supervisor
1909-10	J. A. Cooprider		
1910-11	J. A. Cooprider		
1911-12	J. A. Cooprider		
1912-13	J. A. Cooprider		
1913-14	Noah Oyer Cornelius Dick	J. A. Cooprider	
1914-15	Noah Oyer	J. A. Cooprider	
1915-16	Noah Oyer	Aaron Stolzfus (3 terms) J. L. Shellenberger (1 term)	
1916-17	Noah Oyer	J. L. Shellenberger	
1917-18	J. L. Shellenberger	J. L. Shellenberger	Emily Harder
1918-19	Noah Oyer	J. L. Shellenberger	
1919-20	Noah Oyer	J. L. Shellenberger	
1920-21	M. E. Hostetler	J. L. Shellenberger	M. E. Hostetler
1921-22	M. E. Hostetler	J. L. Shellenberger	M. E. Hostetler
1922-23	M. E. Hostetler	J. L. Shellenberger	Maude Kreider
1923-24	M. E. Hostetler	J. L. Shellenberger	Maude Kreider
1924-25	M. E. Hostetler	J. L. Shellenberger	Mrs. Sam Erb
1925-26	M. E. Hostetler	J. L. Shellenberger	
1926-27	M. E. Hostetler	C. M. Hostetler Geo. Swartzendruber	Students
1927-28	M. E. Hostetler	M. E. Hostetler	

251

A PILLAR OF CLOUD

Year	Superintendent of Buildings & Grounds	Superintendent of Farm & Dairy	Laundry Supervisor
1928-29—J. A. Cooprider	J. L. Shellenberger		
1929-30—M. E. Hostetler	J. L. Shellenberger		
1930-31—M. E. Hostetler	Fred Grove		
1931-32	Fred Grove		
1932-33	Fred Grove		
1933-34	Amos Gingerich		
1934-35	Amos Gingerich		
1935-36	Amos Gingerich		
1936-37	Amos Gingerich		
1937-38	Amos Gingerich		
1938-39	Amos Gingerich		
1939-40			
1940-41			
1941-42			
1942-43	O. O. Hershberger		
1943-44	O. O. Hershberger		
1944-45—Freedley Schrock	O. O. Hershberger	Mrs. Nannie Zook	
1945-46—Freedley Schrock	O. O. Hershberger	Mrs. Nannie Zook	
1946-47—Kenneth King	Valentine Swartzendruber	Mrs. Nannie Zook	
1947-48—Kenneth King	Valentine Swartzendruber	Mrs. Nannie Zook	
1948-49—Kenneth King	Edward Hershberger	Mrs. Nannie Zook	
1949-50—Kenneth King	Edward Hershberger	Mrs. Nannie Zook	
1950-51—Kenneth King	Floyd Miller	Mrs. Nannie Zook	
1951-52—Kenneth King Chas. Greaser (Ass't)	Floyd Miller	Mrs. Nannie Zook	
1952-53—Kenneth King	Floyd Miller	Mrs. Nannie Zook	
1953-54—Kenneth King	Floyd Miller	Mrs. Nannie Zook	
1954-55—Kenneth King Charles Greaser	Floyd Miller	Mrs. Anna F. Classen	
1955-56—Kenneth King Gene Swartzendruber	Floyd Miller	Mrs. Anna F. Classen	
1956-57—Kenneth King Charles Greaser		Mrs. Anna F. Classen	
1957-58—Leon Horst Henry Classen		Mrs. Anna F. Classen	
1958-59—Leon Horst Henry Classen		Mrs. Anna F. Classen	

APPENDIX X

LEADERS OF STUDENT ACTIVITIES

PRESIDENT OF THE Y.P.C.A. AND CLASS PRESIDENTS

Year	President of the Young People's Christian Assoc.	Class Presidents	
		High School Seniors	College Sophomores
1909-10			
1910-11—Paul Erb		John Hilty	
1911-12—Paul Erb		S. N. Nunemaker	
1912-13—Paul Erb		Stephen A. Yoder	
1913-14—Paul Erb		Paul Erb	
1914-15—Noah Oyer		Siddie King	
1915-16—Noah Oyer		Noah Oyer	
1916-17—Noah Oyer		John Detweiler	
1917-18—Noah Oyer		Amos Hinkle	

Year	Presidents of the Young People's Christian Assoc.	Class Presidents High School Seniors	College Sophomores
			—4-year college
1918-19—Paul Bender	Esther Good	M. D. Landis	
1919-20—Paul Bender	Willard Smith	Alexander S. Gross	
1920-21—Paul Bender	Titus Lapp	Gustav Enss	
1921-22—Menno Shellenberger	Joseph D. Graber	Herman Albert Claassen	
1922-23—Samuel M. King	Maurice A. Yoder	Samuel M. King	
1923-24—Irvin E. Burkhart	John Hershberger	Chancy B. King	
1924-25—Irvin E. Burkhart	John Moyer	no graduates	
1925-26—Maurice A. Yoder	Edwin I. Weaver	Milo Kauffman	
1926-27—Andrew Glick	Joseph N. Weaver	Andrew Glick	
			—Junior College
1927-28—Andrew Glick	Floyd Kauffman	Paul Mininger	
1928-29—Paul Mininger	Joe Stratton	Joseph Weaver	
1929-30—Paul Mininger	Arnold Smith	Harold Sommerfeld	
1930-31—Philip Krieder	James Brenneman	Ezra Hershberger	
1931-32—Clarence Bontrager	Carl Roupp	Ralph Bontrager	
1932-33—Vernon Roth	Leroy Bontrager	no college graduates	
1933-34—Vernon Roth	Vernon Roth	no college graduates	
1934-35—George Beare	Sanford King	*6 college sophomores* but no graduation exercises	
1935-36—Gideon G. Yoder	Joseph Y. Yoder	Anna Hallman	
1936-37—Ivan Headings	Robert Garber	Walter Marner	
1937-38—Edward Kanagy	Orie Gingerich	Willard Guengerich	
1938-39—W. J. Dye	Lois Gingerich	Reuben Yoder	
1939-40—Ernest Kauffman	Samuel Janzen	Velma Beyler	
1940-41—Richard Showalter	Ralph Buckwalter	Ethan Horst	
1941-42—Wilbert Lind	Simon Gingerich	Daniel E. Kauffman	
1942-43—Eldon Risser	Leo Swartzendruber	Glenn L. Hershberger	
1943-44—Edward Wiebe	David Lehman	Edward Wiebe	
1944-45—Earl Greaser	Harold Yoder	Wilma Miller	
1945-46—Grace Friesen	Dwight Swartzendruber	Tillie Yoder	
1946-47—Frederick Erb	Delbert Erb	Daniel Stoltzfus	
1947-48—Merle L. Bender	Ronald Graber	J. B. Shenk	
1948-49—Evan Oswald	Lloyd Miller	John L. Fretz	
1949-50—LeRoy Bechler	Gene Swartzendruber	Paul Irwin	
1950-51—Myron Springer	John Zook	Chester Slagell	
1951-52—Joe Kanagy (1st semester) Wallace Jantz (2nd semester)	Charles Kauffman	Merle Springer	
1952-53—Merle Springer	Abner Hershberger	Ray Kauffman	
1953-54—James Kratz	Stanley Boyer	Charles Kauffman	
1954-55—D. A. Raber	Don Weaver	Stanlee Kauffman	
1955-56—Lowell Wolfer	Donald Miller	Russell Shenk	
1956-57—Eugene Garber	Gordon Hershberger	Paul Horst	
1957-58—Earl Eberly	Ivan White	Edwin Schrock	
1958-59—Aaron Martin	Dave Beachy	John Blough	

A PILLAR OF CLOUD

EDITORS OF THE JOURNAL

Year	Editor	Assistant Editor
1909-10		
1910-11		
1911-12		
1912-13		
1913-14	M. D. Landis	
1914-15	J. D. Charles	
1915-16	J. D. Charles	
1916-17	J. D. Charles	
1917-18	Paul Erb	
1918-19	Edward Yoder	
1919-20	Edward Yoder	Anna Loucks
1920-21	Edward Yoder	Guy Hershberger
1921-22	Edward Yoder	Paul Snyder
		Anna Loucks
1922-23	Joe Graber	Margaret Horst
1923-24	Joe Graber	Margaret Horst
1924-25	I. E. Burkhart	Myrtle Erb
1925-26	Maurice A. Yoder	Mary Miller
1926-27	Andrew Glick	Mary Miller
1927-28	Andrew Glick	Paul Mininger
1928-29	Menno Snyder	Katie Reber
1929-30	Paul Miller	Ida Yoder
		Edward Mininger
1930-31	Ida Yoder	Bertha Nitzsche
1931-32	Bertha Nitzsche	J. A. Yoder
	(1st semester)	(1st semester)
	George Holderman	Ivan R. Lind
	(2nd semester)	(2nd semester)
1932-33	Jess Kauffman	Bertha Nitzsche
1933-34	Jesse Roth	Dorothy Kauffman
1934-35	Jesse Roth	Sara Flisher
1935-36	Robert Reist	Gideon G. Yoder
1936-37	Leland Shetler, (1st semester)	Mary White
	Harry Wenger (2nd semester)	
1937-38	Leonard Henard	Mary White
1938-39	David Hilty	Clayton Beyler
1939-40	Lester Zimmerman	Ruth Henard
1940-41	Frank Horst	Esther Swartzendruber
1941-42	Wallace Swartzendruber	Edith Yoder
1942-43	John David Zehr	Alice Buckwalter
1943-44	Paul A. Friesen	Margaret Risser
1944-45	Elsie Zook	Martha Buckwalter
1945-46	Miriam Moyer	
	Lois Buckwalter, co-editors	Elaine Yoder
1946-47	Jane Swartzendruber	Donna Lou Byler
1947-48	Donna Lou Byler	Donald Zook
		Robert Kauffman
1948-49	Barbara Snyder	Virginia Baker
1949-50	Wayne North	Mary L. Weaver
1950-51	Don Swartzendruber	Grace Bontrager
1951-52	Geneva Swartzendruber	Rachel Albrecht
1952-53	Willard Roth	Grace Mininger

1953-54—Juanita Brenneman   Lola Bontrager
                                Melvin Schmidt
1954-55—Melvin Schmidt   David Gingerich
1955-56—Doris Slagell   Betty Wicker
1956-57—Ivan Kauffman   Shirley Kauffman
1957-58—Treva Swartzendruber   Ralph Kauffman
1958-59—Wilbur Birky   Orpha Hartzler

EDITORS OF THE LARK

Year	Editor	Associate Editor
1909-10		
1910-11		
1911-12		
1912-13		
1913-14		
1914-15		
1915-16	J. D. Charles	
1916-17	Paul Erb	
1917-18	Amos Hinkle	Estie Miller
1918-19	Esther Good	Susie Snyder
1919-20	Ezra Stauffer	Ruth Bender
1920-21	Paul Bender	Omar Miller, Nellie Zook
1921-22	Edward Yoder	Anna Loucks
1922-23	Guy Hershberger	M. D. Stutzman
1923-24	Glen Miller	John Hershberger
1924-25	I. E. Burkhart	Myrtle Erb
1925-26	Milo Kauffman	Mary Miller
1926-27	Fred Brenneman	Ruth Bender
1927-28	Joe Weaver	Bessie King
1928-29	Paul Mininger	Phoebe Yoder
1929-30	Paul Mininger	Nelson E. Kauffman
1930-31	Nelson E. Kauffman	Clifford Stutzman
1931-32	George Holderman	Ivan R. Lind
1932-33	Jess Kauffman	Bertha Nitzsche
1933-34	Jesse Roth	Dorothy Kauffman
1934-35	Jesse Roth	Tillman Weaver
1935-36	Walter Marner	Wilbert Nafziger
1936-37	Walter Marner	Arthur Shertz
1937-38	Eleanor Reist	Clayton Beyler
1938-39	Leonard Henard	Millard Lind
1939-40	Edward Kenagy	Millard Lind
1940-41	Ruth Henard	Frank Horst
1941-42	Eldon Risser	Barbara Miller
1942-43	Ralph Buckwalter	Paul A. Friesen
1943-44	Paul A. Friesen	Margaret Risser
1944-45	Lois Buckwalter	Miriam Moyer
1945-46	Elsie Zook	Martha Buckwalter
1946-47	Rosalie Garber	Dwight Slabaugh
1947-48	J. B. Shenk	Martha Buckwalter
1948-49	John Fretz	Wanda Lee Weaver
1949-50	John Mark Yoder	Esther Rose Buckwalter
1950-51	Leabell Troyer	Margaret Glick
1951-52	Dellis Schrock	Twila Stoll
1952-53	Bernice Enns	MaDonna Kauffman
1953-54	Rita Frey	Ardyth Hostetler

A PILLAR OF CLOUD

1954-55—Joyce Gingerich   Velda Miller
1955-56—Donald White   Ellen Penner
1956-57—Ellen Penner   Harold Blosser
1957-58—Duane Miller   Carol Histand
1958-59—Carol Histand   Ivan White

"SCROOGE" IN THE CHRISTMAS PLAY

1943-44—James Greiner   1951-52—Merrill Raber
1944-45—Harold Yoder   1952-53—Paul Unruh
1945-46—Dean Swartzendruber   1953-54—Melvin Schmidt
1946-47—Frederick Erb   1954-55—Melvin Schmidt
1947-48—Delbert Erb   1955-56—Paul Horst
1948-49—Donald Zook   1956-57—Gordon Hackman
1949-50—Wayne Yoder   1957-58—Aden Troyer
1950-51—Clayton Gerber   1958-59—Cecil Miller

APPENDIX XI

SPECIAL BIBLE TERM DATA

Year Instructors	Enrollment
1909-1910—George R. Brunk	16
1910-1911—A. D. Wenger	14
1911-1912—J. S. Hartzler	15
1912-1913—J. S. Shoemaker	17
1913-1914—J. A. Ressler	15
1914-1915—John Thut	20
1915-1916—D. D. Miller (Middlebury, Ind.)	33
1916-1917—A. I. Yoder	24
1917-1918—J. A. Ressler; C. D. Esch	51
1918-1919—S. C. Yoder	57
1919-1920—J. R. Shank	60
1920-1921—S. C. Yoder	42
1921-1922—S. C. Yoder	19
1922-1923—S. C. Yoder	23
1923-1924—Simon Gingerich	19
1924-1925—N. E. Miller	15
1925-1926—J. A. Ressler; J. D. Mininger; J. N. Kauffman	24
1926-1927—Daniel Kauffman	31
1927-1928—J. K. Bixler	24
1928-1929—Regular Faculty	15
1929-1930—S. M. Kanagy	19
1930-1931—John Thut	18
1931-1932—Milo Kauffman	16
1932-1933—1st half—John Thut; 2nd half—J. D. Mininger	56
1933-1934—J. R. Shank; J. D. Mininger	71
assts.: N. A. Lind; Amos Gingerich	

Year	Instructors	Enrollment
1934-1935	J. R. Shank; J. D. Mininger	73
1935-1936	T. K. Hershey; J. C. Gingerich; Jess Kauffman; L. S. Yoder; E. M. Yost	85
1936-1937	Menno Troyer; J. C. Gingerich; S. J. Miller	94
1937-1938	Menno Troyer; D. D. Miller; H. J. King	99
1938-1939	Jess Kauffman; Aaron Mast; L. C. Miller	82
1939-1940	Jess Kauffman; John Thut; Elmer Hershberger; E. M. Yost; J. D. Mininger; J. J. Hostetler	74
1940-1941	Wilbert Nafziger; S. Paul Miller; Harold Brenneman	73
1941-1942	Jess Kauffman; E. J. Berkey; Dr. Fred Brenneman	71
1942-1943	Jess Kauffman; Edward Diener; Dr. Fred Brenneman	51
1943-1944	Jess Kauffman; Ezra Stauffer; Charles Diener; Richard Birkey; A. Lloyd Swartzendruber	36
1944-1945	John Gingerich; A. Lloyd Swartzendruber	33
1945-1946	I. Mark Ross, Dir.; O. O. Hershberger	18
1946-1947	I. Mark Ross; C. J. Ramer; D. D. Brenneman	47
1947-1948	Jess Kauffman; Aaron Mast	78
1948-1949	Laurence Horst, Dir.; Sanford King; Paul Voegtlin; O. O. Hershberger	59
1949-1950	I. Mark Ross; L. S. Weber	44
1950-1951	Laurence Horst, Dir.; Mr. and Mrs. Paul Erb; Dr. Fred Brenneman; Dr. Paul Brenneman	56
1951-1952	Laurence Horst; Harry Diener; I. Mark Ross	47
1952-1953	Milo Kauffman; I. Mark Ross	34
1953-1954	Milo Kauffman; John H. Koppenhaver; John I. Byler	31
1954-1955	Milo Kauffman; George R. Brunk; Milton Vogt	53
1955-1956	Milo Kauffman; George Beare	7
1956-1957	(Special Bible Term discontinued.)	

BIBLIOGRAPHY

SOURCES FOR CHAPTER I

Hartzler, J. E. *Education Among the Mennonites.* Danvers, Illinois, The Central Mennonite Publishing Board, 1925.

Horsch, John L. *Mennonites in Europe.* Vol. I. Scottdale, Pennsylvania, Mennonite Publishing House, 1950 (Second Edition.)

Horsch, John L. *The Mennonite Church and Modernism.* Scottdale, Pennsylvania, Mennonite Publishing House, 1924.

Mennonite Publishing House. Scottdale, Pennsylvania.
  a. *Christian Monitor.* Volumes I, II. January 1909-Dec. 1912.
  b. *Gospel Herald.* Volumes I-III. April 1908 - March 1911.
  c. *Gospel Witness.* Volumes II, III. 1906 - March 1908.
    (Mennonite Publishers then called "The Gospel Witness Co.")

Kauffman, Daniel. *The Mennonite Church and Current Issues.* Scottdale, Pennsylvania, Mennonite Publishing House, 1923.

Peters, H. P. *Education Among the Mennonites in Kansas.* Hillsboro, Kansas. 1925.

Smith, C. Henry. *The Mennonites of America.* Goshen, Indiana. Published by the author, 1909.

Smith, C. Henry. *Mennonites in History.* Scottdale, Pennsylvania, Mennonite Book and Tract Society, 1907.

Smith, C. Henry and Hirschler, E. G. (Ed.) *The Story of Bluffton College.* Bluffton, Ohio. Bluffton College, 1925.

Wenger, John C. *Glimpses of Mennonite History.* Scottdale, Pennsylvania, Mennonite Publishing House, 1940.

GENERAL SOURCES

Early Source Materials

  T. M. Erb, Correspondence and Records
  T. M. Erb, Diary
  T. M. Erb, Notebook

Periodicals

  Christian Monitor
    Mennonite Publishing House, Scottdale, Pa.
  Hesston Academy Journal, 1910-1918
  Hesston College Alumni Bulletin
  Hesston College Journal
  Gospel Herald
    Mennonite Publishing House, Scottdale, Pa.
  Gospel Witness, 1907
    Published by John Funk

Lark (Hesston College Annual)
This Month
    Hesston College

Minutes, Records, Reports, Publicity Materials
    Annual Reports of Administrative Officials
    Annual Publicity Bulletins and Pamphlets
    College Catalogs
    Communicator (Information sheets sent to the faculty)
    Minutes of the Administrative Committees
    Minutes of Faculty Meetings
    Minutes of the Local Board
    Minutes of the Mennonite Board of Education
    Minutes of Student Clubs and Organizations
    Official Notes, 1909-1953
    President's Memo to Faculty, 1953-1959
    Records of the Registrar

INDEX

260